ALMOST IS NOT GOOD ENOUGH

ALMOST
IS NOT GOOD
ENOUGH

HOW TO
WIN OR LOSE
IN RETAIL

ANDREW JENNINGS

First published in 2017

Copyright © Andrew Jennings 2017

The moral right of Andrew Jennings to be identified as the author of this work has been asserted in accordance with the Copyright, Designs and Patents Act 1988.

ISBN 978-1-911195-64-1

Also available as an ebook
ISBN 978-1-911195-65-8

Typeset by Jill Sawyer Phypers

Cover design by Concrete

Printed and bound by CPI Group (UK) Ltd, Croydon, CR0 4YY

Photographic Credits
P2: Saks © Photographer: Jamie McCarthy, Collection: WireImage, Getty Images
P5: Amazon Solar Rooftop © Amazon
P22: Topshop © Topshop/Arcadia
P26: Selfridges © Selfridges
P61: Bon Marche © Le Bon Marché DR
P69: Fortnum & Mason © Fortnum & Mason
P89: John Lewis © John Lewis Partnership
P120: H&M © H&M
P142: Nordstrom © Connie Zhou/OTTO
P162: Woolworths © Woolworths SA
P168/171: Holt Renfrew © Holt Renfrew
P182 Hema © Hema
P187: Primark © Primark/Dalziel & Pow
P214: Ted Baker © Ted Baker
All other photos are credited to John Ryan

This book is dedicated to my grandchildren:
Samuel, Oliver and Joe.

Contents

Acknowledgements   ix

Foreword
      by Ian McGarrigle   xi

Introduction
      Be relevant   1

Chapter one
      The way we shop today   15

Chapter two
      Creating the in-store customer experience   35

Chapter three
      A point of view   55

Chapter four
      Reinventing shopping – the technological revolution   77

Chapter five
      Supply chain revolution   97

Chapter six
      Inventory management   113

Chapter seven
      Talent   131

Chapter eight
      Leadership   151

Chapter nine
      Retail marketing – a visual treat   167

Chapter ten
      Omnichannel   189

Chapter eleven
      International   205

Afterword
      Almost is not good enough   223

Acknowledgements

I could not have completed this book without the assistance and support of many talented and passionate individuals. I would like to express my sincerest thanks to them all.

Firstly, to my wife Karen, youngest daughter Nicole and her husband Pierre, for their ongoing support, love and encouragement at every stage of this production. Also to my talented editor Teena Lyons and my assistant Joanna Becker; I am most grateful for their ongoing professional assistance.

Many of the world's most talented retail CEOs and Chairmen have made terrific contributions to this book, giving their own perspectives on retail relevance. I am most grateful to each and every one of them.

There has also been a large technical team behind this venture, each of whom has helped in their own individual way. Thanks go to Anne Sheinfield, James Bidwell, Karl Gilbert, Matt Clark, John Ryan, Richard Hyman, Ros Barclay, Hannah Channing, Jim Conte, Sucharita Mulpuru, Susan Rose, Marjie van der Walt, John Bond and Nick Bubb for sharing their professional expertise.

I have also been extremely fortunate to have found sponsorship from Paul Martin and the KPMG team and Moira Benigson MBS. Diti Katona and the Concrete Team in Canada have also been hugely generous with their time concerning the design for the book's cover.

Foreword

by Ian McGarrigle, Founder and Chairman, the World Retail Congress

Retail is such a vital sector that it is rarely discussed or debated. It is something that has simply always been there. For years, centuries in fact, it existed to meet people's basic needs. As societies prospered, modern retailing developed to serve not just 'needs' but 'wants' too. New kinds of stores – emporiums even – such as supermarkets, hypermarkets, department stores, convenience stores and many other formats sprang up to sell amazing new products.

But something has happened that is threatening that established view of retail. There has never been such a seismic shift as the one we are currently experiencing. The internet, new technology, social media and an empowered, fickle and less brand-loyal consumer have combined to create a new phenomenon. We now have multiple shopping channels from which we can all shop 24/7 from just about anywhere in the world. As a result, the importance – and therefore number – of physical shops is shrinking. To be a success in retail, new talents are urgently required, many of which are steeped in technology and the digital world.

A question that is often asked by those outside the industry is: Against all these pressures and challenges, why would *anyone* want to be a retailer today?

The answer is quite simple. Retailing has always been an exciting, fast-moving and extremely competitive sector. The challenges vary, but the way to meet them remains largely the same. Success is about being better than your competitors by having the very best offer, great products and excellent customer service. If ever there were a retailer who encapsulates those qualities and that instinctive retail approach then it is Andrew Jennings. I have known Andrew for over 25 years and he is truly a retailer of the world, having run some of the biggest and most iconic retailers across six countries, three continents and two hemispheres. His enthusiasm for retailing has never dimmed.

Andrew constantly travels the world, meeting with retailers in all sectors, including many new start-ups. He believes that to be successful you have to be relevant to your customers. Being relevant requires a constantly enquiring mind, and Andrew demonstrates that belief in everything he does. Andrew's book *Almost Is Not Good Enough* brings together all of his years of knowledge and experience and is truly inspirational. He gives a detailed break-down of how to be successful in retailing today in a guide that should be essential reading for everyone in the business, from young retail trainees to those moving up the corporate ladder to even the very best retail CEOs who are striving to make their businesses relevant and therefore highly successful. Yes, retailing is more challenging than ever before, but it is also more exciting than ever, as this book demonstrates.

Introduction

BE RELEVANT

One of my most abiding career memories centres on the time I lived in New York, working as president of the iconic luxury speciality store group Saks Fifth Avenue. It was December 2004 and, as I headed off at the end of a long day, I confess I was not exactly filled with the Christmas spirit. Indeed, any form of festive celebration was far from my mind. Instead, my brain was wearied by a long series of impending meetings and a heavy workload stretching far into the weeks ahead. I was already mentally totting up what I had to get through the following day.

As I stepped out onto the wintry street of Fifth Avenue, my attention was immediately diverted by a huge crowd. There were hundreds of people crowding the sidewalk, huddled together in their bulky coats and woolly hats, stamping their feet to keep warm. They were all staring intently at the Saks store in front of me. I couldn't help but turn to follow the direction of their gaze, even though I already knew what had caught their attention. It was the huge seasonal display of digital snowflakes across the entire façade of the Fifth Avenue building. The Saks team had really excelled itself that year with an impressive, fully-animated, electronic snowflake set-up, complete with an audio soundtrack that was piped to the street outside. This was the first time customers had experienced anything like this in US retail, I was certain. I heard the crowd break into oohs and aahs of sheer delight as the musical and visual performance reached its peak. I broke into a broad smile. My troubles of a few moments ago were vanquished.

This was what it's all about. If I had forgotten it for a moment, now it all came back to me. For these people, at that instant in time, our Saks store was so much more than a place to buy merchandise. It was a focal point of wonder, delight and discovery.

Today, when anyone talks to me earnestly about 'what needs to be done to keep the retail experience relevant', I often think of that moment. While our retail sector is changing by the day, the central reason why people choose to shop in one place over another has remained the same for years. They choose one brand over another because they love the experience. Any retailer that can find a way to keep the magic will win every time.

Saks Snowflakes light up Fifth Avenue, NYC

Be relevant

In over 40 memorable years in this industry, I have lived through some of the most dramatic changes in retail, from the introduction of the first-ever supermarkets to the invention of the barcode to the advent of online shopping. During this time, we have all changed the way we shop completely. From a time when stores closed at lunchtime on a Saturday until 9.30am on Monday, even the ones in the bustling capitals of Europe, we can now shop 24/7 and have goods delivered straight to our front door at practically any time we please. We've learned a whole new vernacular, with words and expressions such as 'pureplay', 'click and collect' and 'virtual shopping' tripping off our lips with ease. Many people don't think twice about whipping out a smartphone, or even their watch, and buying a must-have item with a couple of swift actions.

While all of this has been progressing, I have been working in a leadership position at many of the world's most respected high-end retailers, from Harrods and House of Fraser in the UK to Brown Thomas in Ireland, Holt Renfrew in Canada, Woolworths in South Africa, Karstadt in Germany and of course Saks Fifth Avenue in the USA. But, even though I have been fully immersed in retail for more than 40 years, I still regard myself as a student of retail. I learn something new nearly every day and love doing so. In fact, I don't just appreciate the changes in my market, I relish them. They are what makes retail such an exciting and fulfilling career.

It is clear to me that the retail industry is currently going through an unprecedented pace of change. Although it has always been a dynamic industry, right now it is experiencing seismic changes that are driven by the changing wants, needs and desires of customers.

Consider this: today one of the biggest retailers in the world, Amazon, owns no stock. The biggest taxi company in the world, Uber, owns no taxis. Meanwhile, the biggest provider of accommodation, Airbnb, owns no facilities. The retail environment has turned on its head in the space of a handful of years.

Economic shifts and breathtaking technological advancements are just two key influences that are changing the retail environment faster than most retailers are able to react.

Take technology as a case in point. Retail ecommerce has experienced tremendous, even exponential, growth. According to statistics from eMarketer, worldwide online retail sales reached $22 trillion in 2016, up 6%

on the previous year, and will top $27 trillion by 2020.[1] In the UK alone, online sales are around £60 billion, and the country is a world leader when it comes to retail ecommerce's share of total retail sales, with its share expected to increase from 14.5% in 2015 to 19.3% in 2019.

Our phones, PCs and tablets are not just important when it comes to buying online. These devices are becoming integral to our decision-making processes when we shop in-store too. According to a survey by Deloitte, more than half of our in-store purchases are influenced by research done online beforehand.[2] In other words, shoppers carefully weigh up all the options before they even set foot in many stores.

To truly appreciate the nature of change on the high streets and in central business districts, compare the shopping journey of the pre-ecommerce age to that of today. Before the internet came along, shoppers might do research by looking in a magazine or catalogue, but most likely they'd get the majority of their inspiration by undertaking some browsing in-store. Once they'd come to a decision, they'd pick up their selection, take it to the counter, pay and then take their goods home. Along the way, they might have a brief conversation with the shop assistant.

Today, from my perspective, that experience is 180 degrees different. The research stage is infinitely more complex. While people can and do still get inspiration from print media and in-store browsing, they will also be inspired by celebrities, web searches, retail mobile apps, dedicated retail websites and digital signage. Word of mouth continues to be important, but equally important are reviews – in other words, 'digital word of mouth'. People want to hear what actual consumers are saying about a product or service, which is why websites have made online reviews a key component of their selling. This research stage is also greatly affected by the algorithms of the major search site (Google) and shopping site (Amazon), and many of the smaller search and shopping websites. These algorithms determine what a customer actually sees and what the site offers its customers.

Voice (the next big technological shift, as exemplified by Amazon's fast-growing Alexa) will even further affect the research stage. On the Amazon website, if I search 'razors', I will be taken to a page (or pages) of multiple types

---

1 Emarketer.com, *Worldwide Retail Ecommerce Sales: The eMarketer Forecast for 2016*
2 Deloitte, *The Deloitte Consumer Review, Digital Predictions 2016*, 2016

and brands of razors with Amazon's recommendations at the top. However, I can scroll through if I want, looking at the different kinds of razors and checking the customer reviews. However, if I say to Alexa, 'I want to buy razors', it will respond with only a very few versions of what's on the website. Those that Alexa spouts out are determined by Amazon's algorithms and/or its immediate business goals. For example, it might want to push its own private-label brand. Voice is the technology of the (near) future, and algorithms will have ever-increasing influence on the customer's research stage.

And, while we are on the subject, let's pause for a moment to think about why Amazon can come up with these fantastic innovations again and again. It has been prepared to invest in vision and growth because it is not fixated on profits. The retailer has completely turned the traditional business model on its head by ignoring profitability – and shareholders don't mind one bit! Every penny they make is ploughed back into the company to produce the next 'wow' factor. And, with the vast amount of money at the company's disposal, those innovations keep on coming at a spectacular rate. That's pretty hard to compete against.

Amazon Distribution Centre

The steady stream of innovations is phenomenal for consumers in a host of ways. Once the modern customer has come to a decision to buy an item, they have a variety of options when it comes to paying for and receiving their goods. There are staffed checkouts, self-service checkouts, mobile payment via your phone or payment through a PC. Purchases can be collected from the counter, delivered to your house, made available for a drive-through pick-up or placed in a secure locker for click and collect. As for our interactions with store staff, the possibilities are seemingly endless. No longer is it a case of a brief exchange at the counter when paying. We can communicate via interactive kiosks, mobile apps, live video, call centres, email or online chats.

Is it any wonder our expectations have changed dramatically?

The consumer is driving the change by demanding ever more convenience, faster delivery and greater choice. Technology giants and retailers have to react at a furious pace, throwing out all sorts of new ideas to see what will stick with consumers and satisfy this desire for something ever more innovative.

With more and more choice at their fingertips, today's consumers crave vastly different and more sophisticated experiences whenever they shop on the high street. They have higher expectations of product, service, value and environment than ever before. If they don't get what they feel they deserve, customers have no qualms about going elsewhere. The net result is that customer loyalty is nowhere near what it used to be: there is no such thing as a 'customer for life' any more. Now that customers can easily access product ratings and store reviews online, social media habits shape where they shop and what they buy, not long-held loyalties. Consumers are no longer loyal to stores or to brands, which will increasingly put branded products at a great disadvantage against Amazon's own private-label products. Oh, and if a retailer gets it wrong, the customer is far more unforgiving than they've ever been before. In fact, research has found that 79% of customers would take their business to a competitor within a week of experiencing poor customer service.[3] A staggering 68% would never return.

For any retailer, this raises some very real questions. Most pertinently: Is it possible to do more than simply survive in the modern environment? Better still, how do we thrive? What is the secret to keeping shoppers coming back time after time?

---

3 AccessDevelopment.com

Be relevant

After many years spent leading retail organisations around the globe, it has become very clear to me that the answer to this question is to **be relevant**.

I am convinced that relevancy is the key to our ongoing success. Remain relevant and customers will return to your doors time and time again. Become irrelevant and you and your organisation will wither and die.

The retail graveyard – as I like to call it – is full of once great businesses that were once relevant but have allowed themselves to become irrelevant. In the year in which I began writing this book, more than two dozen retailers in the UK became insolvent or appointed administrators, including BHS, Austin Reed and Store Twenty One. More than 1,250 stores were affected, as were 24,488 employees. Prior to that, in 2015, the year ended with 25 companies failing, 728 stores affected and 6,845 employees facing an uncertain future. That was a relatively good year in comparison with the previous one, during which 43 large and medium-sized store groups ran into trouble with 1,314 shops and 12,335 shop workers affected.[4] Aside from the obvious human cost and the blight to our high streets caused by boarded-up stores, it is worth remembering retail is one of the most important sectors of the British economy, contributing 5% to GDP.

Irrelevancy doesn't necessarily mean the end. It is possible to turn things around, but it takes some effort, investment and creativity. I've had extensive experience of helping irrelevant retailers to become relevant once more. When I took over the Karstadt business in Germany in 2011, Karstadt had just emerged from insolvency. It was a distressed business that had become irrelevant to its customers. There had been underinvestment in stores and systems. Outdated structures and thinking abounded. When Nicolas Berggruen purchased the business, we put together a plan to make Karstadt relevant once again. It is possible to do this, but it is not an undertaking to be entered upon lightly; it requires deep pockets and long arms. I will go into the Karstadt story in more detail in this book.

---

4   Centre for Retail Research, Who's gone bust in retailing? July 2017

Although it does require sustained effort, being relevant is not complicated. Indeed, I have found there are just four criteria essential to remain relevant:

- Know your customer and understand their emerging wants, needs and desires.
- Constantly innovate – and innovate with excellence.
- Hire talented people who are passionate about what they do.
- Ensure your merchandise assortments are in line with market trends and your customers' needs.

It is no coincidence that *know your customer* is at the top of this list. It is, after all, the customer who ultimately decides whether or not a retailer is successful.

However, this is not something a retailer can tick off and say, 'Yes, I know them and what they want, what next?' My dear mother was a Selfridges shopper. If the iconic Oxford Street store had just retained its focus on making sure her generation was happy, it would have become irrelevant very quickly. Each generation inevitably dies off. It is the natural cycle of life. The next generation always wants something different, though. It is key that a retailer takes the time to get to know what the new generation wants (and then the next generation and the next). This, in brief, is how to remain relevant – though clearly it is not that simple, because consumers' wants and needs change at internet speed. A shopper's view of what's hot and what's not changes on a daily basis. We can never lose sight of the fact our business starts and finishes with the customer.

The customer provides the key to the next item on my relevance list: *constantly innovate*. Winning retailers embrace innovation and change. They're constantly monitoring customer trends, working with suppliers, designing innovative store environments, and conceiving and marketing exciting products and services. I always say, 'Show me an organisation that is innovating with excellence and I will show you a successful business.'

I am concerned that physical retailers don't always take full advantage of cutting-edge technology to devise new methods of customer engagement in-store. Yes, some retailers may understandably be reluctant due to the notoriously thin margins in which this industry operates, especially since they have to pay for fixed costs such as high street rents and labour. However, there is evidence to show that investment in technology and innovation for bricks-and-mortar retailers will produce a commercial return on investment.

Be relevant

The innovations offered by mobile and wireless technology are not exclusive to the tech world and should not be seen to be either. And, never lose sight of the alternative: do nothing and risk sliding into irrelevance. One thing is certain: future multichannel retailers will embrace the latest technology to assist their customers in shopping 24/7.

None of this is to say that retailers should all be investing in technology for technology's sake – the modern high street's version of keeping up with the Joneses. No, retailers need to think about incorporating technology in ways that customers will find engaging and innovative. Again, I have documented ideas here on how retailers might go about transforming a shopper's in-store experience by using cutting-edge technology and experiences.

While it is easy to get swept up in the digital future and all the opportunities it presents, retailers can never lose sight of their most important asset: their people. Retailers still need to focus on how to continually *hire, develop and retain talented, passionate people.*

Payroll costs are undoubtedly a considerable expense for any retailer, and over the years I have had many discussions with CFOs and CEOs about payroll productivity. However, from my viewpoint, having the right staff is key. The right people are the greatest asset for any organisation and you need to pay top dollar for them. This has always been my philosophy.

There is a level of creativity and personal interaction that, for now, only humans can achieve. This will of course change as technology becomes more sophisticated and customer friendly. Now, more than ever, store staff are brand ambassadors. Retailers need to stamp their identity on every touch point with the customer, and their staff are key to establishing and maintaining that connection.

Store staff don't just have to be confined to selling what can be squeezed onto the shelves in-store either. Give them an iPad and they can be the ambassadors for your entire online catalogue too.

Over the years, my fanatical attention to detail on inventory management – having the right merchandise in the right quantities and at the right price – has been a mainstay of keeping the businesses I've worked with relevant. For this reason, I have dedicated an entire chapter to inventory management, which is the lifeblood of our businesses.

Finally, of course, we all need to accept and *embrace change.* There can be no denying it: the retail environment has changed irrevocably and it will go on changing. Customer buying behaviour is altering the entire retail ecosystem. It is fuelled by new businesses and technology that appear on an almost daily basis.

A couple of years ago, a colleague returned from Japan, pumped with a story of a meeting with the chairman of Fast Retailing. A gigantic framed sign dominated the wall of the chairman's office. It said simply: 'Change or Die'. When you think that Fast Retailing operates Comptoir des Cotonniers, Helmut Lang, J Brand, Theory and Uniqlo, this tells you all you need to know about this organisation. These are all hugely successful international retailers. If they can be flexible, then so can our business. It was a good lesson.

No one can stop change from happening, nor should they try. Nor can we accurately predict what might happen next. Not with any certainty, anyhow. I rather like the story about how in 1980 the great minds at management consultant McKinsey were asked to forecast the size of the US mobile phone market 20 years on. The figure they came up with was 900,000 units. The true figure turned out to be 109 million!

Often, embracing change involves a leap of faith (someone has to be the first, after all). It may involve going against the grain, or the perceived advice of the day. When Argos first mooted the concept of 'click and collect' in the early 2000s, customer surveys and outsiders were unanimous that this was not a smart idea. 'Who in their right minds would want to reserve something and then go all the way to a store to pick it up?' they asked. What is the point? Now, as we all know, it has been a tremendous success that has been successfully emulated in numerous stores elsewhere.

We need to think beyond traditions in merchandising, promotional strategies and marketing initiatives. We must embrace the new, however odd or counter-intuitive it feels at first glance. Comfort and tradition are all very well, but they quickly become irrelevant. So, if you are a retailer, brace yourself and enjoy the ride. The bricks-and-mortar store of the future will be filled with discovery, excitement and fun.

Retailers cannot afford to ignore the fact that the consumer of today has changed and is changing. Above all, when customers venture away from their screens and out onto the high street, they want an *experience*, just as the Saks Fifth Avenue crowd so visibly demonstrated.

To be relevant, retailers need to go one step further than the old retail principle of providing the right goods at the right price at the right time and in the right quantity. Without a doubt, the way forward is experiential shopping. Retailers have to learn to be agile, mobile and innovative, connecting with customers in new and novel ways. Offering a unique experience is the best way to grab shoppers' attention when they have made the effort to visit your store personally.

Many retailers might comfort themselves with the belief that they have gone at least part way down the path of embracing the modern shopper by investing in omnichannel capabilities. In other words, most bricks-and-mortar retailers have been savvy enough to know it is no longer enough to simply trade from bricks-and-mortar stores. An online presence is essential in the modern retail environment. However, in too many cases, this is as far as they have gone. The digital and physical operations could be two entirely different retailers. When the online store provides everything the latest technology can offer and the high street store remains static, it doesn't take much to guess which will win the customer. While the way things are displayed and marketed will, of course, differ to some extent between the digital and physical worlds, the customer must clearly understand that it is the same retailer who is operating both channels.

To remain relevant, retailers need to understand the new order. The key is to merge the physical and the virtual. Stores can be turned into vibrant platforms for innovative, relevant shopping experiences that offer something entirely different from online retailers and yet at the same time remain complementary. This is not to say that there is no need for the digital platform to innovate, because of course there is, but simply that the two must work together to give customers what they really want. Likewise, the web experience must seek to offer the best of the in-store experience online.

Fifteen years ago, while I was at Saks Fifth Avenue, we set up a totally separate ecommerce business, which ran autonomously from the bricks-and-mortar organisation. At that point in time, starting from nothing was a relevant strategy. However, once the fledgling business had got off the ground and became a major part of the organisation, it was merged with the bricks-and-mortar store to create an omnichannel business.

This is not an easy mix to achieve, and getting the balance right is a challenge for any retailer. What is the best strategy to prioritise? What happens when the next wave of technology comes along, such as virtual reality or wearable computing devices? How can you become relevant and, most importantly, *stay relevant*?

In this book, I have sought to lay out my criteria for how a retailer can remain relevant in the modern retail world. I have used experiences I have gained through my career in retail and also through countless store visits I have made around the globe. As a keen observer of trends, I undertake regular 'retail safaris' in cities wherever I go. I want to see what works and what doesn't, and am constantly on the look-out for something new. Often it is the smallest boutiques that come up with great ideas and create a real buzz on the high street. I have sought to capture some of that magic here to show how it is possible to remain relevant and bring shoppers back time and time again.

Throughout this book I have included many examples of shops and pureplay businesses that I consider to be highly relevant, along with my explanations of how they have achieved this feat. Plus, since it is also useful to learn from mistakes, I have featured a number of defunct retailers. These are stores that may once have been relevant but that became irrelevant and eventually succumbed to what had for them become inevitable: the retail graveyard. I have sought to identify the errors that were made and offer suggestions as to what these retailers might have done differently, if they were given their time again.

Because two heads, or indeed many heads, are better than one, I have asked some of the globe's top retailers what they feel the secret to relevance is. You will find the unique, informed insights of more than 33 leading retail figures throughout this book, giving an unparalleled snapshot of what it takes to make the grade in retail today.

I have endeavoured to break down the elements that I believe contribute to relevancy, putting them into easy-to-follow subject areas, such as merchandise, technology, customer service, value, marketing, leadership and talent. I have also examined the importance of brands, vision and geography. Each one has an important contribution to make in becoming relevant and sustaining that position, regardless of the advances that happen in the world around us.

As I have found, it won't always be easy to stay relevant; however, it is essential to do so. For one thing, there is a tightrope to be walked where a retailer tries to make sure the merchandise assortments delight customers while remaining relevant to the latest trends and technologies so as to inspire the next generation of customers. Often, that just won't be possible and a retailer will have to make some brave decisions in order to forge ahead and remain relevant. That's the challenge of being a relevant brand: keeping your point of view and at the same time keeping totally focused on your customers' wants, needs and aspirations.

Be relevant

Failure is not inevitable in retail. There is no mythical life-cycle that says all retailers have their day and then simply run out of steam. Yes, failure to react can lead to an inevitable downhill spiral, but there are plenty of stories of once-relevant retailers who became irrelevant and then found their way once more. React properly, find your relevance and you will live to fight another day.

This book is based on what I have learned from working with many of the world's great relevant retailers and from observing others on the high street. Not everything I have done has been a resounding success, but I've learned from my failures as well as from my triumphs. The important thing is: I've never been afraid to try new things. It is my passionate hope that you will find my lessons of interest and will be inspired by these real-life examples from retailers across the globe.

Customers will never desert the high street entirely, but they will increasingly polarise towards the retailers that offer them the experience they love and enjoy. As I found with my experience at Saks Fifth Avenue that Christmas, the stores that find a way to stay relevant will have crowds beating a path to their door. Retailers that find that magic will be around long into the future.

Here's how.

Chapter one

THE WAY
WE SHOP
TODAY

The customer is no longer simply 'king'. Today, as I like to say, the customer is a superbeing! They are the all-knowing, all-seeing and all-powerful. When they venture out onto the high street, or buy online, they are well informed and fully confident. Frequently, they know even more than the retailer themselves about the products they seek to buy.

While much has been said and written about *how* customers shop in the modern era, it is just as important to recognise *what* drives these behaviours. From my perspective, understanding customers is the number one priority for any retailer. Without this information, there is no possibility at all of becoming, or remaining, relevant on whatever platform you choose to sell your goods. After all, it is the customer who makes the final decision as to whether you will be successful or not.

You don't need to look very far to see that the present generation shops in an entirely different way from previous ones. The most obvious manifestation is, of course, the amount of goods we now buy online. Today, 20% of clothing and footwear is bought on the internet and it is predicted this figure will rise to over a third (34%) by 2026.[5] This pace of change has exceeded everyone's predictions. When trading first began on the World Wide Web, the prevailing school of thought was that selling fashions online would never take off to any real extent because consumers would always want to touch and try on clothes. So much for preconceptions!

Timing is, as always, everything. In 1998, a good friend of mine in the USA set up an ecommerce business selling designer fashion. Unfortunately, it was not successful and closed down. It was not because the concept was not correct: the timing was just too early and customers had not yet engaged with the idea of purchasing designer wear online.

Now, of course, buying online is the norm. It is not just e-fashion that is seeing soaring trade either. The online trend is replicated in leisure goods (24% buy them online today and 34% are predicted to do so a decade from now) and furniture and large electrical goods (13% today, 23% in 2026). The same is true of cosmetics and small electrical goods (8% rising to 18%).[6]

Most retailers have accepted the reality of it all and are preparing well for the digital future, offering omnichannel retail opportunities. In other words, customers are able to buy goods from the same retailer both online and in physical stores. I will explore how this can be most effectively done later in this book, but for now let's cast an eye over other key influences on our shopping patterns. Many of these influences are overlooked in the race to produce a seamless retail experience, but to me they are the foundation of everything. They hold the key to relevancy.

Take, to begin with, the changing *attitude* of the modern consumer.

Once upon a time, most families would declare with confidence that they were Tesco or Waitrose shoppers (for example). Yes, geography played a part, since people tend to favour the nearest available supermarket or convenience store, but there was always a sense of what your choice of outlet for your weekly shop said about you. All that has changed in recent

---

5   CACI. Annual Retail Briefing, May 2016
6   CACI. Annual Retail Briefing, May 2016

years. You only have to look at the rise and rise of discount grocers such as Aldi and Lidl. These chains have been dubbed one of the most disruptive forces in British retail, and rightly so. They have been luring middle-class and high-class shoppers away from their familiar stores in droves. No one is hiding away from it either. Most people will proudly tell you how they spent a fraction of their weekly budget on cut-price – but award-winning – wines, dry-aged steak or lobsters.

Convenience stores have become all important for the time-starved customer – a slight retreat to the local corner shop habit of years gone by. People are happy to top up their weekly shop as and when required. The discounters have introduced a whole new shopping style too. They've taught shoppers to seek out 'special buys' or 'weekly offers', which are seemingly random selections of items – from Dyson vacuum cleaners to satnavs to seasonal candles to room fragrances – that will appear one week at a deep discount and disappear the next.

In days gone by, it was not uncommon to see people dressed from top to toe in just one brand. My mother and her friends would never imagine teaming a Max Mara dress with an M&S jacket. It was just not the done thing. It simply didn't occur to them to do anything other than listen slavishly to the advice of sales assistants (who did have somewhat of a vested interest in maintaining this philosophy) or to rely on the security of buying the brand they'd always bought. Today, though, the customer is far more confident in their personal style. They will mix and match brands and price points. It is perfectly acceptable to team a Ted Baker top with a skirt from H&M and shoes from Prada. Finish the look off with a quirky hat bought on a trip to a far-flung country and people will soon be complementing you on your sense of style.

PROFESSIONAL VIEW
How to Be a Relevant Retailer

- Agility and experimentation will be increasingly important as the future becomes more and more unpredictable.
- However, a clear North Star – a mission or purpose – will help you to navigate the future.
- Customer, customer, customer – an old adage, but the only one.

- Retailers must invent! The famous quote attributed to Henry Ford – 'If I had asked people what they wanted, they would have said faster horses' – could not be more appropriate in the current climate.

Paula Nickolds
MD, John Lewis Partnership, International

Much of this change of attitude is a byproduct of the internet age: we are attuned to tapping into new trends faster and demanding more choice. With this choice comes a feeling of power and control, which consumers relish exercising. Plus, with more information at our fingertips, society as a whole is more confident, open-minded and accepting of diverse viewpoints. Or, even if we don't entirely accept different perspectives, we know they exist and are more likely to take them into consideration. Consumers celebrate this harmony in the way they dress, eat and decorate their homes. They feel safe in going to extremes and following their intuition, rather than the crowd. Shopping for 'good, better, best' is now the norm. Who cares if a £3 t-shirt is teamed with a £200 pair of jeans and a £1000 handbag? It's fine as long as the look and feel are right. Similarly, if the discount dry-aged steak tastes first class, why not serve it to your dinner-party guests?

This is not to say consumers no longer care what other people think of their choices. Social influences are as crucial as they ever were and we continue to take our cues from what our peers are doing. Customers today still enjoy making smart, informed purchasing decisions by tapping into their social and familial networks. That is nothing new. What has changed is the nature of those networks. While good old-fashioned word of mouth still plays an important role in the decision-making process, that word of mouth is just as likely to be digital these days as verbal.

Additionally, customers can do more than simply describe a product they like and ask their friends' opinions. They can send pictures or video clips of the item under discussion via WhatsApp, Instagram or Facebook to invite comment. Likewise, those friends can send back their opinions in the same way. Colours, prices and styles can be compared at the click of a button, putting retailers and manufacturers under the microscope like never before.

Again, there is no question about it: the customer is in charge.

Many of the changes we see have undoubtedly been fuelled by choice. Consumers have so much choice today. I am not just referring to the many ways of buying and receiving their goods, but also to the seemingly endless variety of products and services on offer in the marketplace.

Take fashion as a case in point. Our relationship with our wardrobes has been transformed in recent times. We now 'need' considerably more clothes than we did in the 1980s. Most people have far less formal wear, or office clothes, compared to just a decade ago, but will have hangers and drawers full of casual and leisure clothes. We dress differently and are able to come up with a variety of outfit permutations from our apparently boundless closets.

Nearly everyone will admit to spending more than they need to when it comes to clothes. However, thanks to a new generation of low-cost, fast-fashion retailers such as H&M, Primark, Uniqlo and Zara, shoppers have grown accustomed to getting greater value for money. Fashionistas can afford to pop into their favourite store and 'get the look' of any celebrity they like, safe in the knowledge these chains will get the new trends on the rails at a dizzying rate.

Even mainstream retailers have responded to this change. The old cycle of one collection for each season – spring, summer, autumn and winter – is now all but forgotten. New designs appear on a programmed basis. Supply chains have squeezed their production cycles into days rather than weeks. The time to market (the all-important period when garments are ordered and then delivered to stores) for a must-have look has been halved, then quartered and then halved again. This is where traditional department stores frequently meet their Waterloo, especially with their own private brands. They have often tended not to have the in-house expertise, or talent, to offer a competitive, quality assortment with value for money.

Successful fashion retailers are doing more than managing to turn out trend after trend that consumers go crazy for; thanks to aggressive sourcing and supply chain strategies, 'good' and 'better' fashion price points are selling at lower prices than they sold historically. When fashion is perceived as excellent value, customers barely give many of their purchasing decisions a second thought. They'll simply dash into a shop, or use their smartphone, and pick up an outfit for a specific occasion as and when they need it. What could be easier?

This brings us to another important factor in consumer behaviour today: the perception of time. In the 1930s, Cambridge economist John Maynard Keynes predicted that in the future we would only work three hours a day, and then only if we chose to. To be fair to him, economic progress and technological innovations had shrunk working hours quite considerably at that time, so it was a plausible assumption that the trend would continue. However, as we all know, Mr Keynes was completely wrong. Most people feel that they have less time than ever before. We are the 'time-starved generation'.

While there are plenty of time-saving appliances that have taken the drudgery out of our lives and sped up the more mundane tasks, there are just as many that seem to make us more busy. How many people do you hear moaning about the wizardry that chews up their days? Whether it is working through an endless list of emails, keeping up with friends and family via social media or texts, or sitting in a long queue of traffic (albeit in an electric car), technological advances mean our days feel busier and fuller than ever.

Being time starved doesn't mean we are not shopping. It is just that, now time is an increasingly precious commodity, we've been forced to change the way we do things. Spending our time wisely is just as much of a priority as spending our money carefully.

This has had two important impacts on the retail environment. The first is that all retailers need to prioritise making sure their customers feel that any retail transaction is conducted quickly and efficiently and that their assortments are well edited for choice. Amazon has been widely viewed as leading the way in this endeavour. Indeed, the online retailer has taken convenience to a whole new level. It was the first to introduce perks such as one-click shopping and free delivery, dramatically reducing the time between ordering and receiving goods in the process. It introduced the Dash button, where consumers can instantly reorder basic goods – from washing powder to razor blades – with a button press. The retailer is developing revolutionary drone delivery technology to get products even more quickly and efficiently into the customer's home or office.

Many retailers have, not surprisingly, followed Amazon's lead. Developments in technology play a key role in offering a hassle-free shopping experience to consumers who are (ironically) short on time thanks to, well, technology. Any bricks-and-mortar retailer that hopes to remain relevant needs to be on top of self-service tills, cashless payment technology and high-tech in-store navigation.

Technology can be used in an infinite number of creative ways. Christopher Bailey, the talented fashion designer behind the success of Burberry, has changed the time of his biannual runway show from afternoon to evening so that more customers around the globe can experience a live stream in-store, select their product and make their purchases immediately.

See it, like it, buy it. Other retailers have now developed a similar approach.

Online, the service needs to be seamless, from beginning to end, with clearly defined terms for delivery and returns. Retailers are offering ever-quicker delivery terms: as little as an hour for many.

CROWD PLEASER *Moda Operandi, USA*

Moda Operandi was the first luxury e-retailer to allow its customers to watch a fashion show online and then pre-order from the designers immediately as the show ended so they received their items without delay. Not surprisingly, this unique pre-order model has attracted exceptional interest from exclusive designers and discerning customers alike.

Customers want things as fast as they can get them, which is why Moda Operandi has been such a success.

There is a second impact to be felt from keeping one eye on the pressures of time. As well as offering a seamless shopping trip, retailers need to make sure that, if a shopper chooses to spend their valuable time in a particular store, or on a website, every single moment is believed to have been well spent. This, to me, brings us to one of the most crucial aspects of relevance: the customer experience.

PROFESSIONAL VIEW
How to Be a Relevant Retailer

- Look forwards, never backwards.
- Absorb, interpret, act.
- Never stop moving – preferably forwards.
- Remember that it's not what you do, it's what your competitor does. They may be moving faster than you.

Lord Stuart Rose
Chairman, Ocado, UK

Consumers today are all heavily under the influence of what is known as the 'experience economy'. This means there has been a huge shift in behaviour away from enjoying spending our spare time *buying* things to preferring to spend it *doing* things. Our appetite to collect for the sake of collecting is waning. In its place is a heartfelt desire to live in the here and now and make the most of the spare time we have. This is why we are spending a higher proportion of our income on holidays, cars, entertainment and eating out. 'Have less, do more' is the oft-heard cry of Generation Xers and Millennials. It's all about servicing a lifestyle rather than simply buying goods.

This trend translates into a growing expectation that a visit to a store, or website, should be about more than a simple transaction. Consumers – who receive so much mental simulation elsewhere – will no longer feel satisfied by simply picking up their chosen product, plonking it into a basket and paying for it. They want added value. They crave an experience. If consumers don't feel this expectation is met, they will go elsewhere.

The most successful retailers are those that offer time-poor shoppers experiential value when they shop. Everything they do is about making their particular retail destination *the* exciting place to be. Any retailer that attracts people on this basis won't just guarantee they'll keep shoppers with them for longer; they'll also be in pole position to capitalise on what can be a store

Topshop Oxford Circus, London

group's greatest potential profit stream: the impulse buy. If shoppers can be encouraged to linger in a particular store for longer and feel well disposed to the retailer, they will spend more. Guaranteed.

RELEVANT RETAILER *Topshop, International*

Five reasons the Top Shop flagship store in Oxford Circus, London, is a customer favourite and very relevant:

Great assortment

Whether customers are after celebrity ranges from Kate Moss, Cara Delevingne or Beyoncé, the biggest range of accessories in town (the flagship store in London's Oxford Circus turns over approximately £5 million a year in costume jewellery), or boutique, vintage or leisurewear collections, the range is perfectly suited to its entire customer base and expertly curated.

Constant newness

Topshop is the master of understanding exactly who its core customer is and constantly offering them new things to maintain their interest. The store introduces hundreds of new designs each week. Now it is even possible to watch videos of its catwalk shows and buy a selection of styles immediately. How's that for being up to date?

A hotbed of discovery

You could easily while away an entire day at Topshop's flagship store. If you want a tattoo, you can have one. You can also have your eyebrows threaded, your body waxed or your nails done. If you need a break from shopping, there are eateries, and anyone partial to cupcakes will be in heaven during a visit to the dedicated cupcake counter. All of that is before you even explore the myriad ranges of fashion and accessories on offer.

It's personal

Topshop has zeroed in on a highly personalised service that helps customers to hone and refine their own styles to perfection. Shoppers can have their denims embroidered, or patched, in any style they like. Selected stores offer a completely free personal shopping service. Customers simply book an appointment and receive one-on-one style advice on the latest in fashion, all in the comfort of a private dressing-room suite.

And fun too

Giant video walls, photo booths for those all-important group pictures when shopping with friends, and frequent in-store events reinforce the retail-is-entertainment message.

Experiences are not just about having a good time either. Done well, the retail experience can also offer something else that is vital in the modern world: a sense of community. Visiting bricks-and-mortar stores is one of the ways we get out of the house and meet other people in an era when so much social connection is done online.

Human beings are neurologically wired to connect with one another. The high street or shopping mall is a place where we can interact at the same time as learning about products and brands. It switches the role of shops from a place where we simply go to buy things into one where we enjoy meaningful social interactions. Shopping is frequently combined with trips to restaurants, cafés, leisure centres and cinemas. Relevant retailers ensure they are an integral part of that experiential visit.

CROWD PLEASER *Lululemon, International*

This yoga apparel store dedicates roughly one third of its 11,500-square-foot store in New York's Flatiron District to a concept called Hub Seventeen, a community gathering place where shoppers can take yoga workshops, view art and films, and attend concerts. The store also offers a concierge service to help shoppers book an exercise class or find a running route in the Big Apple.

Yet, while customers crave experiences and community, it is not the case that one size fits all. No, to add another ball into the juggling act retailers already need to perform, consumers also demand to be recognised as individuals, rather than part of a homogenised group. It is not enough to have an experience. Consumers want a *unique* experience. Personalisation is another significant element in the mix that drives the way people want to shop.

This should not come as a surprise to any retailer. After all, everyone likes the personal touch. Whether it is the local coffee shop remembering you like a skinny latte with just a light sprinkle of cinnamon or a website helpfully suggesting a jacket you might like to go with those trousers you bought last month, the thoughtful touch goes far. My daughter Nicole, who lives in Australia, recently received an email from Witchery fashion store with wardrobe suggestions to match a top she had bought the day before. Helpful photos of garment suggestions accompanied the email.

PROFESSIONAL VIEW
How to Be a Relevant Retailer

- The next 10 years will be a golden age for those who can offer real richness and depth across the virtual and physical realms.
- Selfridges wants to make itself and the world we live in sustainable. When it comes to inspiring change in social and environmental issues, our actions speak as loud as our words.
- We champion creativity, providing moments of retail theatre that cannot be experienced elsewhere.
- Cultivating communities, creating valuable connections and building strong relationships will enable us to drive positive change both within and outside our business.
- We understand that shopping transcends the perfunctory. We make decisions with our emotions, understand nuance and subtlety, and know the meaning of special and desirable because we feel it in our bones.

Anne Pitcher
MD, Selfridges & Co, International

Personalisation, where products are carefully curated and branded for a specific customer, is hot today. It is becoming more popular to have clothes embroidered with names and initials (see the Topshop example on page 24) or to have monograms added to bags, pens, cufflinks and even Christmas baubles. My benchmark for personalisation in the UK is Selfridges, Oxford Street, and in particular its Christmas assortment. Every festive season the store offers a fantastic personalised range: everything from chocolates to lingerie to champagne to glassware to wrapping paper. I think I counted 50 different options when I visited in 2016.

Selfridges, London – Hall of Wonder

Personalisation doesn't just need to mean individual branding of certain types of goods. On a wider level, it may mean targeting merchandise to specific customer groups. A retailer may cater to petites or to a particular geography, or may take into account regional variations or nuances. Shops in Florida might have a 52-week-a-year beach department, for example. International retailers can 'personalise' their assortment according to the tastes and expectations of their customer bases in specific geographies. I was visiting a retailer in Cairns, on the northeast coast of Australia, in winter (July) 2016 and the temperature was 30 degrees Celsius. It had boots and winter shoes in its shoe department but not a flip-flop or sandal in sight. While this might have been appropriate for Melbourne and Sydney, it certainly was not right for the milder winters of northern Australia.

As many retailers have discovered, providing that personal touch isn't just playing lip-service to the latest trend; it is an important marketing currency.

CROWD PLEASER *Helly Hansen, Norway*

Global sport and leisure firm Helly Hansen uses geo-targeting to personalise the shopping journeys of its customers from Norway to Spain. The homepage of its website alters according to the local weather conditions experienced by the shopper accessing the site. Thus, during a five-day spell of rain in southern Germany, the local page switched from promoting skiwear to rainwear. This led to a sales uplift of 170%. Product descriptions are also localised, so 'trousers' and 'jumpers' in the UK are translated into 'pants' and 'sweaters' in the USA.

As the Helly Hansen example also shows, retail businesses, like consumers, increasingly operate on the international stage.

Today, more than ever, globalisation is at play. Customers can buy international brands online and are far more savvy about where their favourite products come from. This also means they are alert to many more ideas and enjoy the element of discovery they've learned through their travels. Any retailer that can emulate at least part of that experience will tick the right boxes with the adventurous modern consumer.

While trying to understand the motivations of the contemporary shopper, it is worth highlighting that we are dealing with three different generations. There are the Boomers, who are reaching their sixties and seventies in the 2010s, and at the other end the Millennials (also known as Generation Y), who are aged between their late teens and their mid-thirties. Generation X falls between the two. We must also not forget Generation Z: this even younger, emerging generation generally lacks brand loyalty and appears to be more interested in experiences. While many of the attitudes discussed in this chapter are common to all four groups, each one has its own habits and attitudes.

Millennials, for example, have a tendency to be far more sensitive to stores and brands that they feel have a social conscience and 'give back to the community'. They like their purchases to have meaning or some sort of ethical consideration. They are more likely to err towards organic produce, or goods that are linked with projects that, say, invest in needy communities or plant a tree for every purchase.

Gen X shoppers are generally more down to earth. What motivates them is high quality at the right price: it's OK if it costs more, as long as the quality is good and it is value for money. This explains the success of brands such as Made.com, which sells affordable, stylish and good-quality furnishings thanks to its business model, which eschews intermediaries. Interestingly, the more cynical Gen X are less influenced by community-orientated or environmentally friendly messages, although they do prefer transparency and consistency when they make their choices. This group, more than any other, prefers niche or personalised products that they believe most reflect their personality.

The Boomers are an interesting bunch too and certainly should not be written off as 'past it' or stuck in their ways. Apart from anything else, they have more disposable income than the generations that follow. They are young at heart; indeed, the Boomer generation feels more youthful than any comparable generation that has gone before. They want to spend their disposable income on anything with an emphasis on maintaining this youth and vitality. And, in a spot of good news for physical stores (which are so used to playing catch-up with digital these days), Boomers often purchase their goods in-store rather than online.

Above all, the customer of today – whether Gen Z, Millennial, Gen X or Boomer – is very discerning. In the main, they don't mind where they go, providing they can get the product they want, at the right price, and enjoy the experience at the same time. For the real icing on the cake, customers want to:

- be the first to hear about new products,
- know where to get the best value for money and
- have a clear line of communication with the retailers they are buying from.

There is no doubt about it, the evolving needs and desires of retail customers are shaping and reshaping our sector on a daily basis. Any retailers hoping to make a mark must deliver a compelling range of merchandise or services in the most convenient, efficient and compelling way possible. Failure to recognise this will put any retailer on a downward spiral towards the retail graveyard.

RETAIL GRAVEYARD *BHS, UK*

Five reasons why customers fell out of love with BHS:

Ageing customer base

Each generation has its own needs, wants and aspirations as well as its own unique point of view about the world around them. As BHS's customer base aged, the store simply aged with them. The older generation has firm expectations about a fixed price point, leaving no room for change or growth. BHS never aspired to serve, or refocus towards, the subsequent generations. Unless a retailer is totally focused on who its customer is and how to inspire new generations of customers, it will become irrelevant. The store will die off with the customer base.

Tired stores

With little or no revenue growth, BHS compounded its problem by failing to invest in its stores or technology. Many shops became tired, tatty and down at heel.

Dated menu

Even the menu in its cafés and restaurants dated BHS. It was still serving bangers 'n' mash long after most eateries had switched to healthier and more cosmopolitan options.

Inconsistent ranging

At one stage, BHS had a reputation for being the place to go for lighting and home furnishings. It was also strong in Christmas gifts. Unfortunately, these areas were beacons of promise in an otherwise dull sea of clothes, children's and accessories. The message was inconsistent and customers were quite rightly confused about what BHS stood for.

Unchanging

There was no excitement in-store. One discount offer followed another. It felt like time had stood still in many of the product ranges and store layouts. A customer seeking to replace the BHS trousers they had bought a year earlier could go to the exact same place in-store and pick up the exact same style of trousers. Where is the fun and experience in that?

So, does all of this mean that none of the old rules apply when it comes to customer service? Does the customer of today expect an entirely different type of service to reflect their new expectations? The answer is an emphatic *no*. The old standards still apply, and then some. You can offer all the bells and whistles in the world, in terms of choice, experiences and time-saving, but if you get the basics wrong – the core elements of customer service that have been in place for more than a hundred years – you may as well not have bothered.

Good customer service is about the entire shopping experience. Whenever I think of customer service, I always remember a conversation with Isadore 'Issy' Sharp, the founder and chairman of the Four Seasons hotel group in Toronto. He once shared with me: 'Andrew, with every interaction in our hotels, we polish the brand or we tarnish it. Every single interaction, from the bell boy, right through to the maître d', plays its part.'

The basics of customer service were set in stone long before we had ever heard of the internet, or became time poor, or obsessed by choice. By tradition, the very best customer experience runs from the way we are met and greeted as we enter the retail premises through to being served and thanked for our purchases and then wished goodbye. Indeed, to me, the final metre of the customer experience, as I like to call it, is still the most crucial of them all. This is where the shop assistant hands the goods over to the customer, or better still (if appropriate for the retailer) comes around to the other side of the counter to deliver them in person. This is where people make up their minds about a store and where the rubber really hits the road.

Customers have not changed so much today that they no longer value great customer service as an important part of the retail experience. Indeed, it is still a significant part of the appeal of a physical store and should not be forgotten in the dash to appeal to the modern customer. In my view, online retailers must also seek to emulate as much of the traditional customer service magic as possible within the confines of technology. Engagement starts on the website or a phone. If the customer cannot find the information they are looking for, this can be perceived as poor service. As always, retailers should make sure all goods, in all sizes or permutations, are in stock, all the time. There is nothing more frustrating, or likely to drive shoppers into the arms of a competitor, than being informed, 'sorry we do not have that size' or 'we have just sold out of that colour'. I have a favourite lounge-shirt brand that is sold in selected speciality stores. It sends me crazy when I go into a particular store to be told, 'sorry that is our most popular size and we never have it in stock'. Having everything in stock is a key part of customer service and it needs the full attention of senior management. In any business that I am associated with, management sets 'never out of stocks' in the top 800 stock-keeping units at 99%. Technology is hugely helpful too, when it comes to offering to deliver that out-of-stock item to the customer's home or office the same day.

If you have excellent merchandise availability, the rest of the customer experience can happen and you will remain relevant.

RELEVANT RETAIL TIP

It is worth noting here that some retailers have become quite savvy about out-of-stocks and have even trained their customers to accept them! Let me explain.

When I was group MD of Woolworths South Africa (a premium retailer), we had a hugely successful high-end food business. If a particular product was out of stock due to our supplier not being able to attain the quality we required for fresh fruit (e.g. raspberries or strawberries), our customers would accept this and buy an alternative. During the peak trading season (e.g. Christmas or Easter), when the demand would be greater than the supply, savvy customers would just come in earlier. It became something of a cult and not seen as negative. By presenting its food as fresh and finite, Woolworths South Africa made a virtue of being out of stock if the quality was not 100%.

Health warning: *this will only work if the customer is confident in the retailer, the standard of its products and its quality–value equation.*

Whether online or bricks and mortar, shops should always make the returns process as straightforward as humanly possible. My personal view on refunds – and I have a strong one on this topic – is that it is a cost of doing business that retailers need to account for in their business models. It is far better to 'hug the customer' and give them peace of mind than to become consumed with petty nitpicking over returns. My benchmark in the retail world is the Nordstrom organisation, which has a no-quibble returns policy. Over the years I have had numerous discussions and debates with store management teams about this contentious subject. I believe you create more goodwill by not arguing about returns. I must point out that serial return customers need to be dealt with in a different way, as it is not acceptable to return a ludicrous amount of merchandise, but my experience has shown that customers like these are few and far between.

Another aspect of the basic customer experience that is critically important is the fitting room. I am sure that anyone reading this will have heard at least one fitting-room horror story and may even have one of their own. You know the scenario, where the poor customer is standing in their underwear, making a silent prayer that the store assistant will return sometime soon, so they can ask for a larger size or different style. I'm frequently astonished at how many stores I've visited where there appears to be no one responsible for fitting rooms at all.

In all stores, a basic fitting room needs to be hygienically spotless and have appropriate lighting. Lingerie fitting rooms, in particular, need softer, more forgiving lighting, with somewhere to sit and mirrors where customers can view the back of a garment. Designer fitting rooms should have more space to accommodate mother and daughter or two friends, and digital mirrors to record the outfits so views can be sent to friends online. My benchmarks for the best store fitting rooms are Harvey Nichols in Birmingham (UK) and the personal shopping department in Saks Fifth Avenue in New York (USA).

Again, this is a customer service basic that will never go away. There is no point following any of the advice on relevancy in this book if these basic items are not attended to first. Sadly, many retailers do not get this point. I will include some further ideas on this in chapter four.

The way we shop today

As I hope this chapter has illustrated, my strong view that the customer is, without a doubt, a superbeing. Remember, customers can shop when and where they want, demanding ever more choice, and, as if this were not enough, they want to enjoy every single moment too. They also demand transparency, needing to know how much goods are being sold for and how much competitors will charge for the same thing. However, while attitudes have changed markedly in recent years, fuelled in great part by the digital age, this does not mean that the traditional appreciation of exceptional customer service has disappeared. The long-held principle of service – the right goods, in the right place, at the right time – is as pertinent today as ever.

Relevant retailers are those that understand that tailoring their merchandise assortments and shopping experience to reflect their understanding of a customer's lifestyle, preferences and shopping habits is the most effective way to instil loyalty and forge long-term profitable relationships. It is a challenge that requires greater efficiency, innovation and differentiation, and the challenge must be met by every store on the modern high street – whether physical retailer, online or a combination thereof – because only the most relevant retailers will survive.

PROFESSIONAL VIEW
How to Be a Relevant Retailer

- We are constantly trying to see around corners in the road ahead and predicting what's going to be cool, desirable and relevant in our job. The clues are all around us. We just need to truly open our eyes.
- In today's world, we need to innovate in everything all the time. There is no room for complacency.
- Through all the technological, social and environmental changes in the world, we have to be true to who we are to stay relevant. Our core brand essence and DNA have to shine through at all times.
- Retail relevance requires the core of who we are as retailers: resilience and adaptability.

Euan Sutherland
CEO, SuperGroup Plc, International

CHAPTER CHECKOUT

✓ The customer isn't just king, they are a superbeing: fully informed, fully confident and fully prepared to walk away from any shop that doesn't produce the goods.

✓ There has been a huge shift in behaviour away from enjoying spending our spare time *buying* things to preferring to spend it *doing* things. Customers today prioritise experiences.

✓ Pay attention to the basics of retail. The need for them is as pertinent as ever.

✓ Customers today are time starved and need their store shopping experience to be pleasurable.

✓ Your brand must always remain authentic.

✓ The retail graveyard is full of once-relevant brands that have become tired, dated, unchanged and only attractive to an ageing customer.

Chapter two

CREATING THE IN-STORE CUSTOMER EXPERIENCE

I have often said that some people change when they see the light and others when they feel the heat. While you can't always control what happens, you can change your attitude towards it and in doing so you will be mastering the change, rather than allowing it to master you. Retailers who choose to wait until they feel the heat are playing with fire.

As we have already seen, the modern customer demands unique retail experiences. Buying decisions are complex, involving a variety of factors from quality to style to brand considerations, all weighed up against the important metrics of an enjoyable experience that suits the lifestyle of the time-conscious consumer.

In this chapter I would like to focus on what can be done to make each customer's experience unique and memorable within the physical store environment. The online options may differ and will be covered in more detail in chapter ten.

At a very basic level, offering convenience and ease through the physical shopping experience should be a given for any retailer. The future of any high street store or shopping mall hinges on its ability to efficiently serve all of its customers and ensure they get the product or service they need in a timely and efficient manner. It is not unreasonable to expect stores to do all they can to facilitate this, from planning the layout, lighting, signage and product displays to employing an optimum quantity of well-trained, well-motivated, passionate staff who will fully understand the wants, needs and desires of the customer.

PROFESSIONAL VIEW
How to Be a Relevant Retailer

- Don't just meet but exceed customers' expectations with metaphorical 'hugs'.
- Develop personal relationships with customers by really getting to know them so they become your friends forever.
- Use technology and data to develop constantly updated customer personas that tell you who a customer is, what they like and what they've bought.
- Sell with integrity all day, every day.

Jack Mitchell
Chairman, Mitchells Stores, USA

But how do modern retailers create the 'wow' factor? Retailers that wish to become (or remain) relevant need to rethink the retail experience from a customer's perspective. This means developing a business model that seamlessly blends physical, virtual and community experiences, all centred around the customer.

To achieve this goal, retailers of the future need to be what I have termed '3D-mensional'. The three Ds of 3D-mensional are *differentiation*, *distinctive* and *delivering*. Let's take each of them in turn.

Differentiation

Customers have neither the time nor the inclination to give retailers a second chance to make a first impression. They want them to get it right first time. They want reasons to give them their business and to be reminded every time they visit that the retailer not only 'gets' what they want but is also able to deliver it better than anyone else.

Now, more than ever, differentiation is everything. Relevant retailers offer a shopping experience that makes them stand out from the competition and that customers find irresistible. They make their stores exciting destinations where they connect with customers through a distinctive visual environment, unique product pairings or turning a shared moment into a gateway for exciting experiences.

CROWD PLEASER *Pret a Manger, UK*

The sandwich chain Pret a Manger has a philosophy of continuing to challenge itself to keep from going stale. In any given year, at least 10% of its sales come from new products and it is not afraid to innovate or step away from its core business. In 2014, Pret opened one of its London outlets in the evening. The lighting was turned low, jazz music was played and a drinks list of wine and beer appeared. The 'Good Evenings' opening, from 6pm to 11pm, was a one-off trial, but it was indicative of the firm's thinking.

In 2016, Pret launched a completely vegetarian store in Soho, London. The pop-up store was not simply targeted at those who eschew meat but also serviced the healthy-eating boom, which is pushing up veggie food sales in Pret's traditional outlets by 12% per year. Although initially just a four-week trial, Veggie Pret is now here to stay with two stores in London and plans underway for other meat-free stores.

A retailer that has arguably made differentiation an art form is Apple. When founder Steve Jobs first envisioned a physical store dedicated to his iconic technology, his goal was to create an entirely different type of shopping experience. Famous for his fastidiousness and extensive attention to detail, Jobs oversaw the design of an Apple Store format that holistically created value around that experience.

Jobs finally delivered his vision and the Apple Store chain launched just after the turn of the millennium. Key elements in the store's offer are:

- iconic, 'clean' open-space formats where customers can mingle;
- simplified, easy-to-navigate merchandising design;
- competent, engaged and enthusiastic staff who benefit from an extensive training programme on how to interact with customers and do not focus on the 'sell';
- extensive availability of in-store products, loaded with all relevant apps and technology, so customers can experience them in the exact way they will eventually use them;
- Apple Genius Bars, which offer an all-round service for Apple products on a one-to-one basis, are free of charge and can be booked online.

Without a doubt, when it originally opened, the Apple Store looked like nothing else on the high street.

When it comes to differentiation, retailers have three key areas to focus on that might present their primary point of difference. These are:

Merchandise selection

This includes the types of product to be sold in-store, the extent of the various ranges on offer and the quality, value and price level they are pitched at.

Process

This encompasses anything and everything to do with the actual sales process, from the location, layout and look and feel of the store itself to how the payment is managed and how goods are delivered to or collected by the customer.

People

Here, the retailer needs to focus on the customer–employee equation, rather than the process or product, to achieve the desired outcome (the sale). This means getting into the minutiae of the interaction between the store staff or online interface and the customer at all stages and includes the experience from both the staff and the employee point of view.

I feel strongly that marketing is *not* one of the key elements of differentiation. A retailer can conduct the glitziest, most award-winning campaign ever known, but that won't distinguish it as a consistently successful retailer. Marketing is what *tells* the customer about the points of difference and entices customers to shop at a particular store. It should also go without saying that if a retailer says one thing and the reality turns out to be quite different, then the retailer is heading towards the retail graveyard fast. A good friend of mine sums this up very aptly: advertising can potentially bring a poor merchant to a speedy demise.

In years gone by, a large number of retailers sought to differentiate themselves through product selection. A fashion retailer might have decided to target the mid-market with carefully curated ranges for the 40-to-55 age group. Or, a grocer might have carved out a niche in the organic health food section. The internet has opened up the market to literally thousands of small and medium-sized sellers who can bring any and all of these products to our front doors from all over the globe at any time we like. Internet retailers such as Amazon and eBay are also selling an ever more varied selection of goods. Distinguishing oneself solely via product selection is getting harder and harder to do, particularly for physical retailers.

The 'people' and 'process' components present numerous opportunities for differentiation and for achieving that magic, particularly in a physical store. A retailer may differentiate through extraordinary customer experiences, in-store activities such as live-streamed fashion shows, unique entertainment and digital events, or one-to-one interactions.

PROFESSIONAL VIEW
How to Be a Relevant Retailer

- Always put yourself in the mind's eye of the customer. How would I feel (what would I expect) if I were the client, customer or guest?
- Be relentless in establishing with your service personnel the right mix between my 'golden rule' (the how) and clear, consistent expectations (the what) of the technical delivery of service of your business.
- Be equally as relentless, passionate and consistent in the enforcing of your expectations at all levels of staff membership and leadership.

Accountability exists all the way up to the very top of the organisation. This will establish the culture not only of the service your company provides to its customers but also of the company itself.

- Repeat the first three points every hour of every day and search for accomplishment and success stories. Celebrate the good while correcting the bad.

Wolf Hengst
Former Global President, Four Seasons, International,
and Executive Chairman, Six Senses, International

When I took over the leadership of Holt Renfrew, Canada, the store was becoming increasingly irrelevant and less attractive to a younger customer. I spoke with our merchants and discussed the need to bring far more newness, excitement and discovery into the fashion area. The result was the creation of what became known as the Holt Renfrew World Design Lab. It was featured in the store atrium and across two floors, with products covering womenswear, accessories and cosmetics. We featured everything from young international designers through to local design talent from the Ryerson School of Fashion in Toronto. The department was a showstopper and gained a reputation as an area of discovery and newness and as the place to shop for something unique and different. Each Saturday, young designers from Ryerson would be featured. This was a key differentiator and was hugely successful in attracting a young and fashion-forward customer.

Over Christmas 2016, Galeries Lafayette in Paris pushed boundaries at its annual in-store event with the creation of Noël Extra Polaire. Created by technology experts Sky Boy, the Noël Extra Polaire event transformed Galeries Lafayette into a virtual fairy-tale ice field by overlapping animated images with the reality of the actual store-scape. Sky Boy's unique technology enabled virtual images to sit alongside the physical environment with far greater precision than even augmented reality allows. Visitors to Galeries Lafayette needed only to look at the screens of their smartphones or tablets to see a 360-degree polar landscape appear. The magical vision even appeared on balconies and under the ceiling domes so as to maximise the Christmas experience. Galeries Lafayette provided a dedicated space at the heart of the store, along with hosts, to guide visitors through the event. One particular advantage of this event was that the images could be shared via the internet. Thus, the event happened not only in the physical store space but also everywhere outside of it via social

Creating the in-store customer experience

networks. For Galeries Lafayette, Sky Boy's Noël Extra Polaire was as much a retail success as it was a virtual one.

Retailers can give their staff exceptional training and knowledge so they can offer specialist one-to-one advice that people simply can't find elsewhere, even online. Getting the people and processes right gives a retailer a whole host of tools with which to engage with customers. And, as we know, anything that creates that all-important unique wow factor puts a retailer one step closer to being relevant.

Heritage meets Designer at Liberty, London

RELEVANT RETAILER *Liberty, UK*

Five ways in which Liberty has differentiated itself and has a distinctive point of view:

Discovery

Nestled in the heart of London's West End, Liberty is a wonderful store of discovery, delight and surprise that appeals to all of the senses. As you walk through the store, with its numerous nooks, crannies and 'secret rooms', you will suddenly experience the most intoxicating aroma of scented candles or herbs. While the lighting is seductive in some areas, it will pull you up short when it is shocking in the next. Throws and textiles are casually draped over bannisters and handrails, inviting shoppers to touch or stroke them. Every room reveals a new and pleasurable curiosity.

Imaginative use of space

The mock-Tudor building Liberty occupies could be seen to be a disadvantage because of its size and shape, not least the dozens of small rooms and steep staircases within it. However, rather than gut it to maximise selling space, the store has made a virtue of its uniqueness, using the confined spaces imaginatively to add to the air of discovery. This is a large part of what makes a visit to Liberty so special.

No rules

Nothing in the Regent Street venue conforms to the traditional notion of a department store. Liberty has a well-curated yet eclectic assortment of speciality goods, from textiles to kitchenware to artwork to cosmetics. Yet it doesn't seem cluttered, and everything in the range appears to fit together and match.

Chic visuals

The product ranges are displayed in the most creative fashion. There are no fixed features or standardised shelving or rails. Some display items are nailed to walls, while others are hung on stepladders or slung on an old-fashioned gypsy cart, or even suspended on giant springs. Even standard items such as light fittings are used to display yarn.

Creative windows

Windows are a store's number one vehicle for advertising, and Liberty always prioritises its innovative displays, which match and complement the magic in-store.

While it is crucial for any retailer to work out its stance when it comes to product, process and people, and to deliver an experience like no other on the high street, it is impossible for a retailer to be all things to all people. This is why we need the second D of 3D-mensional: distinctive.

PROFESSIONAL VIEW
How to Be a Relevant Retailer

- Never believe you know better than your customers.
- Keep listening to them.
- Focus on what you can be famous for.
- Always strive to continuously improve.

David Kneale
CEO, Clicks Group, South Africa

Distinctive

To be truly relevant, retailers must choose their primary competitive position, or unique selling proposition. I always call this a 'point of view' and it is so crucial to relevance that I have dedicated the whole of the next chapter to it. Just to touch on it now, though, in this context, the point of view is best described as the personality, the character and the vision of the business.

This distinctive character will be in the fields of merchandise, marketing, store design or ecommerce. It is impossible to be all things to all people. Many retailers have tried this and all have failed in the attempt. I always say: what you don't have in your assortment is sometimes as important as what you do have.

Retail businesses must make a conscious choice about what they stand for and stick to it. Thus, a retailer must have excellence in presenting its customers with a truly exceptional range of products, have exceptional and memorable customer service, and create extraordinary retail spaces. Without settling on that single, key point of view, a retailer will not stand for anything. Sadly, many don't. The result? Mediocrity, which leads to the retail graveyard.

Whichever point of view is chosen, the holy grail for any retailer should be to create an in-store concept that is so different and compelling that it renders irrelevant others who are attempting to conquer the same space. In the companies I worked with, I was always utterly clear about the offer and what the company stood for. In other words, there was no question in my mind, or the minds of my customers, what the company's point of view was. It was then the leadership's role to cascade this through the various organisational channels.

CROWD PLEASER *Eataly, International*

Eataly is a completely new food concept, developed in Turin, Italy, and opened in New York City off Madison Square Park in 2010. By 2017, it operated in 31 locations worldwide and counting, each celebrating Italy's rich dining culture. Eataly is not just a market selling top-quality Italian food. Thanks to its unlikely blend of food store, farm stall, educational centre, museum and environmental credentials, it has emerged as one of the busiest shopping destinations and tourist attractions in each area in which it opens. Visiting Eataly is so much more than 'going to a store'. It is an opportunity to shop, eat and learn. This is why customers fall in love with Eataly.

This epitomises a distinctive business for me.

If the primary distinction is strong and the retailer is a market leader, it is possible to introduce further elements to help the retailer stand out from the crowd. These elements complement the main vision. Thus, if the main focus is on price and the retailer achieves dominance, they might also prioritise product selection or process. This primary and secondary strategy would certainly describe what happened with Apple Stores. Having perfected the process side of things with its ambitious store layout and methods of product delivery, it tackled the people side of things by prioritising great service.

I would reinforce that if a secondary priority is added, it is just as important that a retailer meets and exceeds the quality standard here too. If a chain says it is going to wow with its super-slick technology and its fantastic customer service, it had better deliver the quality–value equation as well. All retailers must constantly maintain and nurture their product element. Getting just one element wrong will drag down everything else because consumers will (perhaps rightly) judge that that store is inconsistent and not up to the job.

Prioritising one element is not an excuse to forget all the rest either. Retailers must always meet and exceed the market standard across the board, whether in terms of staffing, store layout or merchandise selection. What we are talking about here is not simply exceeding in one, or two, particular areas. If there is any sign that the retailer falls below the high standards expected in its niche, then it can be as distinctive as it likes in a single area but customers will not be impressed.

There is an infinite number of different strategies available to retailers that wish to stand out from the crowd, and this is why retailing is such an exciting and challenging place to be. If, for example, store design and layout are identified as one of a group's points of distinction, another retailer might opt to break away from such a uniform store design model. After all, there is nothing more depressing, uninspiring and frankly boring than row upon row of uniform shelves and rails stacked with product (I call this 'Rack City'). Imagination is the key to planning eye-catching, thought-provoking layouts. Retailers should not be afraid to do something different, because the more distinctive the store, the more customers will remember it. Look at Ted Baker!

Alternatively, if 'people' is the path chosen, retailers might like to take a leaf out of the book of the Mitchells business in Connecticut, USA. They don't see their staff as an expense that drags down annual profits. They see their staff as a great asset.

Whichever path a retailer chooses, it should always remember how effective the elements of surprise and delight are when it comes to bringing customers in-store. Consumers love the element of surprise. It leaves them with something worth talking about and that adds value to their life beyond the items for which they initially came in-store.

CROWD PLEASER *10 Corso Como, International*

You never know what to expect when you enter 10 Corso Como in Milan, Seoul or Shanghai. The store was founded in 1990 as an art gallery and bookshop and today the shopping and dining complex sells works of art, fashion, music, design, cuisine and culture. It is like a modern theatre in the way it constantly reinvents itself. It is, however, the merchandise that always plays a starring role. Corso Como themes its stores around hot items – say, the best of Prada, or a hat by Philip Treacy, or the latest digital device. The merchandise becomes the magnet that pulls the store together with its own scene and set of characters. The proprietors act as editors, capturing the imagination of customers.

I would always visit Carla Sozzani, the founder and inspiration behind Corso Como, on my biannual visits to Milan. Carla would be my radar and inspiration for what was new in art, fashion, music, design and cuisine – and of course my team members would benefit when I returned.

If you are on the trail of great, distinctive, speciality stores in Europe, à la Corso Como, I have a few more recommendations.

One favourite and a frequently visited store is Leclaireur, rue de Sévigné, Paris. This was the first concept store in Paris and has now been established for over 30 years. I call it the 'radar of fashion' and it is undoubtedly the new direction to follow. Leclaireur is an installation where reality and illusion constantly interplay. It is not just a shop: it is an experience for art, bags, home, décor, jewellery, shoes, perfume, and men's and women's clothing.

My other top tip for most distinctive speciality store in Europe is Biffi in Milan. Rosy Biffi has skilfully combined the great passions of all members of the Biffi family, together with those of her talented staff, to create the winning formula for a business that is renowned and appreciated all around the fashion world. Since the 1960s, many unknown designers, both Italian and international, have found success with Biffi. A guided tour through the store with Rosy was always a memorable experience.

When I was group MD at Woolworths in South Africa during the latter part of 2007 we spent much time building and developing a distinctive food business. One of my focus areas was the development of special-occasion food. We decided that we would build and own a reputation for the very best edible delights for Christmas, Valentine's Day, Easter, Mother's Day, Father's Day and Halloween. We scrutinised every element, including packaging, product innovation and marketing. Our teams spent hours on this and it was crucial to the success of the business. We became the first choice for all special occasions: no competition could touch us.

PROFESSIONAL VIEW
How to Be a Relevant Retailer

- The key role of a leader is to inspire people to embrace change and to take on any challenge.
- You should be customer obsessed, not competitor obsessed.
- The offline and online store is where it all happens and the rest of the organisation should support and serve.
- Create the best multifunctional leadership team, with people who could take on your role one day.

Tjeerd Jegen
CEO, Hema, Europe

RELEVANT RETAIL TIP

Choose your point of distinction, but plan it well and don't overdo it! Burberry started getting itself into real trouble around the turn of the millennium after it licensed its distinctive check too far, expanding it into far too many products with similar looks and feels to each other. It was seen on everything from baseball caps to disposable nappies for dogs, and the upmarket brand became known as the uniform of choice for yobs and football hooligans. Management took quick action to contain this trend and redirected the hugely successful brand.

Creating a strong individual vision is not easy. It takes both commitment and a willingness to change – all of which brings us to the final D: delivery. How does a retailer deliver its distinctive vision?

Delivering

Differentiation is only meaningful if customers can see it, feel it, taste it and experience it throughout the organisation *every* time they shop in a store and at every interaction. Without it, any retail offering is weak and bland.

Real differentiation and distinction mean relentlessly stating what you stand for and how you stand apart from others.

Take IKEA as a case in point. The Swedish furnishings giant firmly follows a clever circulation strategy with its big-box stores: everything is about maximising the customer experience.

It's no accident that the first thing a customer encounters at the entrance to each store is a mountain of yellow and blue shopping bags. The bags are cleverly introduced as early as possible. Thereafter, customers flow around the well-curated store, which is laid out to help them pass each and every decorated room setting. Then, with no sign of an exit in sight, the customer is obliged to walk through a marketplace offering modern furniture and decorative home accessories. If you are in a hurry, as I have been in the past, you may get a tad frustrated as you weave your way around the store of discovery until you reach the checkout. However, the strategy is of course to hold customers all the way from the front door right through to the checkout. At each turn of the meandering route around the store, the customer is assailed with products at various price levels, curated in room sets, on shelves or boxes, or piled high in seemingly chaotic heaps that scream 'here is a bargain!'.

Hardly surprisingly, almost 100% of IKEA customers buy more than they originally planned. Every step of its process design is aimed at maximising potential sales and reflecting its core values, which are honesty, affordability, solutions, inspiration and surprises.

While any retailer would be advised to start off by deciding on their vision, point of view and strategic plan and then putting all of their energies into ruthless execution, it is important to point out that all retailers will, more than likely, develop this outlook over time. Indeed, most of the more successful retail concepts evolve, rather than arriving out-of-the-box perfect. All retailers that set off with one burning vision will quickly find certain things gain traction while others fall by the wayside. That's the beauty of the creative industry that is retail.

Take the example of IKEA detailed above. While the furnishings retailer has firm views on merchandise and layouts, and detailed manuals are supplied to each staff member on exactly how the store is set up, it constantly evolves. The concept of flat-pack assembly, where the onus falls on the customer to build their own furniture when they get home, came about in exactly this way. According to the company's history, the idea of outsourcing assembly appeared when a customer asked an IKEA employee for assistance in removing legs from a table in order to get it into their car. In an instant, a new concept and method for delivery was born and the ubiquitous flat-pack soon followed. Indeed, customers don't simply make their own furniture; they also have to personally go to the IKEA 'warehouse' first to collect it. How's that for a slick concept?

All retailers are in a great position to experiment and constantly try out new concepts. Chains with multiple locations can refine concepts on a regional basis, while large stores can experiment with concessions to trial new products and garner customer reactions.

A case in point is the ongoing popularity of off-price malls, which are now responsible for 75% of US clothing sales.[7] In the past, retailers have used an outlet strategy to fuel growth, but many now use them successfully to introduce their brands to a younger audience. Indeed, a Boston Consulting Group study found that, of the 33% of customers who buy a luxury item for the first time at an outlet, 85% of them are likely to buy a full-priced item from the same brand down the line.[8] Not surprisingly, off-price is no longer dismissed as cannibalising full-price stores. In recent years, Gap, Hugo Boss and Michael Kors, to name but a few, have expanded their outlet store networks. In Europe, Value Retail has delivered double-digit sales growth every year since its first outlet, Bicester Village, opened in 1995. This is against an overall retail sales growth of a sickly looking couple of percent.

The important thing is to evolve (and go on evolving). Customers rightly expect that forward-looking retailers will deliver their products and services in the fastest and most convenient way possible.

---

7   NPD Group. Checkout Tracking. July 2016
8   Boston Consulting Group, *Outlet Shopping Comes to Town*, 2016

CROWD PLEASER *Dover Street Market, International*

Dover Street Market, owned by Japanese fashion brand Comme des Garçon, is a unique collection of fashion boutiques and an eatery under one very avant-garde roof. It opened in the former Burberry store on London's Haymarket in March 2016. The large, century-old, Grade II-listed building presented challenges but founder Rei Kawakubo embraced and enhanced the building's foibles by making them part of the design. The idea was to create an idea of 'beautiful chaos', where the various brands that inhabit the five floors of the market present their own individual style within an overall strong vision – just as customers have their own strong style statements. An eclectic mixture of fashion and accessories is displayed on an even more eclectic mixture of fixtures and fittings, from a child's playground (complete with climbing frame and slide) to industrial ducting thrown into service as clothes rails. For me, a once-a-month visit to Dover Street Market is a must. I finish off the visit with a trip to the top-floor café for a piece of the best carrot cake in London.

Dover Street Market, London – a unique collection of fashion boutiques

Creating the in-store customer experience

Their Tokyo store, which I visited in early 2017, is a good match for London. I was blown away by the distinctive point of view of this store on the Ginza.

Changing things will often take courage. It may even be hard to convince other people that it is the right way to go. This was something I found when I made significant changes to luxury speciality store Holt Renfrew Canada, where I was president between 1998 and 2004. At the time I joined, Holt Renfrew was not as financially successful as it could have been and my vision and that of the owner, Galen Weston, was to turn Holts into a modern world-class store of discovery and delight. The process-driven strategy included completely updating merchandising and point-of-sale technology, bringing in new, exclusive brands and rebranding the organisation.

One of the first barriers to this vision was the restaurant in the flagship store in Toronto. It was a large space and, at first glance, it might have looked pleasingly busy. Look closer, though, and it was clear that most customers were managing to make a single cup of coffee last three or more hours as they sat and gossiped with friends. Some customers even had the audacity to bring in their own wine and champagne! Worse still, I discovered that many of the people who used the spacious café as a meeting space never even shopped at the store.

This did not fit in with our vision at all. I decided we needed to close the restaurant and open it with an entirely new eatery in a new location. I made an arrangement with the talented French artisan baker Lionel Poilâne, who became a good friend until his untimely death in 2002. He would fly us supplies of his magnificent *pain Poilâne* three times a week and the Holt Renfrew restaurant was transformed into an innovative eatery – an appropriate environment for this new concept. (Characteristically, Lionel even assisted in the design of the new eatery.)

Customers were initially furious when we closed down the old established restaurant for its refurbishment. They were even less impressed when they heard what we were planning to do. We feared there would be a riot. At the same time, we knew that if we did not change and modernise we would never be able to fully move the business forward.

When the restaurant reopened as a *tartinerie*, I was greeted with a line of people who wished to complain. I offered them complimentary glasses of wine and a Poilâne *tartine*. Several accepted this and enjoyed it; others never returned. However, we attracted an entirely new group of younger customers. These customers not only bought our food and drink – which they loved, driving the restaurant's profits up by six times the previous amount in as many months – but also enjoyed and shopped in the main store. The new customers were brand conscious, affluent and aware of current trends: in other words, exactly the sort of customer we were hoping to attract.

I had a similar experience when I took the chair role of the legendary, yet failing, high-profile Hema brand in the Netherlands in 2015. We focused on delivering a new, fresh Hema and hired CEO Tjeerd Jegen with the mandate to be an agent of change and to deliver an updated Hema. I could not believe the brand loyalty of the customers in the Netherlands towards Hema; however, it needed a fresh vision.

Just two years later, Tjeerd and his talented new management board had delivered a dramatic increase in profitability, updated merchandise assortments and a decrease in stock levels. They had also launched an innovative loyalty programme and upgraded the brand's omnichannel experience. Hema is now appealing to a modern customer and offers great value for money, sparkling design and great quality. Often, you need to take bold steps. Doing what you have always done and expecting different results is indeed a sure route to irrelevance.

PROFESSIONAL VIEW
How to Be a Relevant Retailer

- Selling what customers want to buy and doing so in an interesting and engaging way: that's relevance.
- The very essence of customer-centricity is relevance. You're not customer centric if you're not relevant to the customer.
- The pursuit of relevance leads to ever-increasing personalisation, from a generic offer to localisation and ultimately to personalisation.
- The pinnacle of relevance in mass-market retail is personalisation at scale. Once this was unachievable, but now it is within reach using data and technology.

Richard Umbers
CEO and MD, Myer, Australia

CHAPTER CHECKOUT

✓ Stand for something meaningful or you stand for nothing.

✓ In creating the customer experience, retailers need to think on a 3D-mensional basis: differentiation, distinctive and delivering.

✓ Don't just meet but exceed customer expectations with metaphorical hugs.

✓ Delivering a consistent customer experience is key.

Chapter three

A POINT OF VIEW

In retail, if you don't stand for something, you stand for nothing. No one walking into Fortnum & Mason would ever mistake it for Selfridges or Debenhams, and vice versa. If I blindfolded you and took you into an American store, you'd know you were in Macy's Herald Square, Bloomingdale's 59th Street or Saks Fifth Avenue the moment I took the cover from your eyes. Everything from the store layout to lighting, audio, visual merchandising and collateral material gives huge clues as to where you are. All of this is a retailer's or brand's point of view.

To be relevant, having a strong point of view is from my perspective non-negotiable. Struggling retailers may struggle for many reasons, but they will have one thing in common: a failure to define their point of view.

A point of view is your declaration of identity to your customers. It is what your brand is all about. It's the equivalent of a large sign that says: 'come on in if you like sophisticated/quirky/modern/bargain (delete as applicable) goods, but walk on by if that is not what you want'. Retailers can never be all things to all people. You don't need *every* customer; you need the customers you are targeting for your business.

John Lewis (UK), for example, has a strong point of view that is all about being 'Never Knowingly Undersold'. Everyone also trusts the policy of Never Knowingly Undersold, fully understanding the fact that they will not pay more for a product at John Lewis than elsewhere. If it is more expensive, John Lewis will reduce its price. The founder, John Spedan Lewis, set this in motion in 1920 and it is just as relevant in 2017.

The department store chain has made customers its first priority and understands that the people reaching out to those customers are its staff on the front line: the employees *are* the company in the eyes of the customer. Thus, John Lewis empowers its staff to live the brand. Not only do staff get a share of the profits and decision-making powers over the running of the company but they are also looked after with a number of exceptional staff perks and bonuses. Ask anyone what they like best about John Lewis and its odds-on they'll pretty soon mention its exceptional customer service. Everyone will have a story about how a partner (as staff members are called) has gone above and beyond and made their shopping experience exceptional.

Elsewhere, stores such as Walmart, Asda, Aldi and Lidl have decided their distinction is pricing and never miss an opportunity to flag up their low prices or the good value of their merchandise. Their stores are a sea of marketing collateral declaring their special offers. Meanwhile, Japanese brand Muji has taken the process route and everything it does, from the store layout to the fixtures to the checkout, is all about simplicity, humility, calmness and self-restraint. The chain, which sells no brands, prides itself on being anti-glitz, in a bid to appeal to those shoppers who are beyond buying brands because they value sustainability and fair trade.

I read a great description of this strategy by business author and commentator Joe Calloway in his book *Becoming a Category of One*.[9] He said no business should strive to be a leader in its category. It is far more effective to create a different category altogether and be the only one in it. That is, to me, a very powerful statement, and I went on to invite Joe to

---

9   Joe Calloway, *Becoming a Category of One* John Wiley & Sons, 2003

speak to my Group Conference when I was president of Saks. I was very keen that he got this message across. The way to get a retailer to the next level of performance is to create something so individual and so special that the customer seeking out such an experience would not dream of going anywhere else. Why would they?

A retail business that has a strong point of view has a clear sense of what it is. It doesn't just define itself in terms of what it sells – whether that is food, designer handbags or homewares – but in terms of what that retail space or website means to customers. Whether it is the composition of the merchandise assortment; the way the merchandise is presented; the quality of the fixtures, fittings and lighting; or the attentive, knowledgeable customer service, everything is dominated by the drive to further that point of view. The focus is never about simply driving the bottom line. This is not to say that retailers need to be charitable and give it away, but simply that they know success comes out of understanding the greater purpose. That is what will drive the bottom line.

Having a distinctive point of view is what protects us all from an undignified race to the bottom price-wise. Think about it. As I have already noted, we live in highly competitive times. The high street is a busy place and there are hundreds and thousands of online stores, all vying for a slice of everyone's cash. Money can easily become the prime consideration when choosing a product.

'Oh, look, I can get it £10 cheaper at selleverythingcheap.com.'

On this basis, the only way to compete is for other retailers to cut their prices by £15 to get the business. Then, there will always be another shop that will go down by £18. Before you know it, prices are spiralling down at a dizzying rate and margins are cut to the bone, if indeed there is any margin left at all.

At issue here is a situation where customers only ever see retail outlets as a means to an end. A commodity. The obvious solution for any store is to rise out of this category and differentiate itself in such a clear and powerful way that customers feel compelled to shop there.

RETAIL GRAVEYARD *Woolworths, UK*

Five ways in which the UK retailer suffered and eventually failed because it was missing a point of view:

Failed to keep pace with changing market

Woolworths traded for more than a century on its reputation as a low-cost variety store. Somehow, though, it failed to notice that other retailers, predominantly supermarkets, were gradually picking off its strong categories, from confectionery to toys to entertainment.

Promise of good value eroded

At the same time as rivals picked off its categories, others began to chip away at its low-price promise. Younger, fitter upstarts, such as Poundland and Wilkinson (now Wilko), did what Woolworths did, but better.

Lack of newness

Even though taste for its core product base and price proposition were shifting, Woolworths did not follow the trend. Even when people openly began to ask what the store stood for, the chain still did not react.

Little investment in stores

With little spare cash, the chain was not able to invest in stores, making them seem down at heel, grubby and forlorn. Customers could buy cheaper products elsewhere and shop in a more pleasant environment.

A point of view

Too reliant on promotional offers

Woolworths built much of its strategy on offering loudly flagged discounts and deals. While this increased sales in the short term, it eroded profitability and also created a negative, 'bargain basement' persona.

Once a retailer has a point of view, it must maintain it diligently and guard it at all costs. I remember when this was vividly demonstrated to me one Christmas when I was running Karstadt. The German retailer's point of view was firmly in the 'family-friendly' territory. Its philosophy was all about being an interesting, warm and welcoming environment for all generations to shop together. Among its extensive range of festive offerings, Karstadt always had a thriving calendar business, and this year was no different. I had gone into the Düsseldorf store early one Saturday morning to check on how the early preparations for the seasonal displays were coming along. Satisfied that everything was beginning to look suitably festive and attractive, I stopped by the calendar department. What I saw there brought me up short. In the centre of the display of calendars, which depicted everything from the latest pop stars to cute pets to charming landscapes, were a series of extremely lurid calendars featuring large nude photos of models in highly suggestive poses. After speaking with the staff in the department, I contacted the buying executive responsible for stationery.

'Are we a family department store?' I enquired, getting straight to the point.

'Yes, we are,' was the reply, with the executive sounding a little perplexed by the call.

'In that case, do you think nude calendars are right for this family image?' I went on. Before the executive had a chance to reply, I continued: 'I have asked the staff on the floor to take them off the shelves. However, I would very much like you and your boss to come and see me first thing on Monday. I really want to know how this fits our point of view.'

The following Monday a very sheepish buyer and buying executive arrived in my office. They both agreed the nude calendars didn't fit the bill as family-friendly merchandise.

The hapless buying executive is not the only example of such careless caretaking of a store's point of view. I've lost count of the number of earnest-looking buyers who have insisted they can sell crateloads of this, that or the other, if only I'll give the go-ahead. The fact remains: if the product in question doesn't fit my store's point of view, I will always veto it. I'm quite sure that, given the right promotion, it would be possible to sell boxes of baked beans in a high-end department store, but that doesn't mean it is a good idea. It may feel like a risk to walk away from a strong-selling product, but if it does not match the point of view it is a false economy.

PROFESSIONAL VIEW
How to Be a Relevant Retailer

- Develop a unique customer experience, creating a destination that embodies a unique point of view.
- Focus on people (employees and customers). For employees, there should be a strong emphasis on management training and mentoring programmes. With customers, satisfaction is *the* first priority.
- Invest in non-commercial events to develop the business so it is not just a shopping destination. Cultural and artistic exhibitions and events that create traffic and work well to deliver a strong message.
- Focus on innovation and new territories, as well as the architecture and store design that are at the heart of the customer experience.
- Remember that we are retailers and we are a brand – not simply real estate managers.

Patrice Wagner
Chairman and CEO, Le Bon Marché Group, France

A store's point of view is everything. It is who it is and how it tells its story. You could even say it is the 'promise' to the customer, and sticking rigidly to that point of view signals a store's willingness to keep that promise. If my Karstadt customers believed in the fact that we were a family-friendly store, we needed to fulfil our side of this bargain – in everything we did.

As my experience shows, a point of view needs to be constantly nurtured and protected to sustain it. But, first things first: how do you define a point of view?

In many cases, it is the owner of a store, or CEO, who first defines its personality. It is a reflection of what this person loves and values.

Bon Marche, Paris – Authoritative and chic Shoe World

CROWD PLEASER *Maison Assouline, International*

Prosper Assouline has, over the past two decades, revolutionised the notion of a coffee table book, creating elaborate, expensively bound volumes of illustrated tales on everything from luxury cars to fashion to architecture. His boutiques in London, New York, Paris, Venice and Geneva reflect his exquisite style and are a truly bibliophilic experience. The Piccadilly flagship store serves espresso and champagne, which can be sipped while sitting on rich antique furniture surrounded by weighty tomes. Like a cathedral to high culture, Maison Assouline's shelves feature selected antiques and there is an 'Emperor's Table' dedicated to one-off exhibitions, such as a tribute to the art of entertaining by Valentino Garavani.

Assouline, London – A truly bibliophilic experience

While Prosper Assouline created his brand as a reflection of his own undeniable good taste, his is not a purely self-indulgent strategy. His focus is 100% on his customers. He knows all about the Assouline shopper. He understands their lifestyles, how they like to fill their homes, how they spend their time and the way they relate to their peers. In the planning of his stores, he has sought to become closer to his customers than any other comparable retailer. The styling of each and every Assouline store reflects his ambition and by doing this he keeps like-minded people engaged. This engagement is achieved through the location of the store, the internal layout and design, the choice and attitude of the staff, and the promotions used to market the brand. Every detail is planned with emotional connection in mind.

Of course, one of the most important aspects of point of view is the merchandise being sold, as my calendar experience showed. The best way to establish, reinforce and emphasise a point of view is through a crystal-clear vision on merchandise. I am constantly walking stores, looking at products and asking myself whether they harmonise and advance a retailer's point of view. I mentioned the Burberry baseball caps earlier. We were selling hundreds of them at Holt Renfrew, Canada, but Rose Marie Bravo, the smart Burberry CEO, decided to remove them from sale as they were being worn by football hooligans and did not fit the Burberry point of view.

PROFESSIONAL VIEW
How to Be a Relevant Retailer

- Define a clear retail proposition and focus on it – ruthlessly!
- Remember the customer is in control – they have huge choice and want to engage with the retailer at a time and place of their choosing.
- Don't expand too quickly.
- Hire only good people.

Peter Williams
Chairman, Boohoo.com, UK

If, as a retailer, you've never really considered the importance of a point of view, there is no time like the present. Think in terms of your key customers: What is it they like about your stores? What is your competitive advantage against other, perhaps similar, stores on the high street that may sell largely the same products? Compare your store to another selling broadly the same category of goods. What is the clear point of difference that a customer sees that will make them say, 'Great, I will choose you.'

If you are not 100% sure, break it down:

- How are you editing your merchandise assortment to create a point of view?
- What are your core values as a business?
- What about your stores matters to you and your colleagues?
- Why should your store or website matter to others?
- What excites customers about shopping with you?
- What makes your retail business different and a leader in the marketplace?

You don't need to try too hard. Retailers shouldn't be thinking in terms of gimmicks as their point of view where, say, stores are decorated in bright lemon paint or staff all dress up as film stars. A point of view could be as simple as selling distinctive, well-edited, quality products, in a well-laid-out, accessible store, with top-notch customer service every time. The answers to the questions above will provide useful indicators as to what makes a store stand out.

What follows is a list of retailers that I believe have strong points of view. It is by no means exhaustive, but it is a useful exercise to think about shops in this way.

Retailer	Point of view
Boohoo.com, UK	Great fashion of the moment at a great price
Costco, International	Lowest prices everywhere
Hamley's, International	Magical, memorable and fun toy world experience for children
Hema, Europe	Modern variety store offering great value, sparkling designs and superior quality
John Lewis, International	Never knowingly undersold: trustworthy quality and great service – a family store
Lane Crawford, Hong Kong	High-quality speciality stores for the best designers
LUSH, International	Edited, eco-friendly and socially responsible beauty and bath
Liberty, UK	Distinctive, well-edited, quirky speciality and decorative home store for men and women
Primark, Europe	Fashion and basics at the lowest price points
Saks Fifth Avenue, USA	Distinctive high-end purveyors of quality designers in beauty, men's and women's fashion, and accessories

A point of view

Selfridges & Co, UK	Very focused fashion department store; constantly innovating with excellence and always at the cutting edge
Victoria's Secret, International	Young, sexy and fun lingerie and beauty
Ted Baker, International	Distinctive and energised of-the-moment men's, women's, children's, home and travel

By contrast, focus on any of the stores that are listed in the 'retail graveyard' sections throughout this book. Think about their point of view. I'm prepared to lay money on the fact you won't be sure what it was in any of the cases featured. Whether it was BHS (UK), Woolworths (USA and UK) or Comet (UK), none of these stores had an updated point of view that resonated with a modern customer – and it showed.

It should be said here that it is a lot easier to have a clear point of view when you are just dealing with one particular store rather than a large chain. Many of the retailers I most admire for their rock-solid point of view are single stores, or at the least store groups with a remarkably strong flagship. I've already mentioned Fortnum & Mason and Selfridges, but there is also Le Bon Marché in Paris, Bergdorf Goodman in New York, Illum in Copenhagen, and TsUM in Moscow and St Petersburg, to hat-tip but a few stores with a phenomenally single-minded point of view.

But what of a retailer with a chain of stores. Does each individual store need an individual point of view? Or should one, overarching point of view span the entire store group, regardless of where each store is located? There is no easy answer to this and I would say that both options have been shown to work. Uniqlo, for example, is a master of creating its point of view, which is almost identical in every shop you visit, from Berlin to Bluewater (its store on Fifth Avenue, New York, may be the only exception). Its striking proposition of innovative, high-quality, eye-catching products at affordable prices is reinforced at every turn. There is something quite reassuring about being wowed by a familiar 'wall of cashmere' at whichever branch you wander into.

Other chains, particularly those that operate on an international basis, might opt for a regional point of view. There will be more about this in the international chapter (chapter eleven) later in the book.

RELEVANT RETAIL TIP

As an aside, a point of view can be an effective lens to review what I call the 'thick middle' of stores. Pretty much all significant-sized chains suffer from it, especially in the department store world. This is a rump of marginally profitable stores that limp along from one year to the next, without ever really contributing a huge amount to the bottom line. In the majority of chains, there are a minority of stores that make the majority of the profit – the 80/20 principle.

The truth is, the only solution to a thick middle is to tackle it!

Retailers need to be ruthless with their businesses and cut back on the store portfolio in areas where it is clear that a particular store will never be relevant. However, this is also the area where having a good idea of the point of view can entirely change the fortunes of many in the thick middle. I recommend taking some time to get to know the customers who shop at the 'thick middle' stores and see whether sufficient is being done to offer a memorable experience, whether in terms of merchandise assortment, lighting and layout, introducing innovative eateries to increase dwell time, or better still all of the above. This is a major issue for all department store groups and it will become a death knell if not tackled in time.

Analysing the point of view of the portfolio is always my first step upon joining any new retail business. I want to know exactly what the business stands for. If I believe the point of view is weak, it is my priority to find the most powerful and appropriate one and then reinforce it at every turn, whether it is across individual shops or the chain as a whole.

This is something I did when I became president of Holt Renfrew in Canada. When I joined the fashion speciality group, it had stores throughout Canada with questionable profitability. Looking around the stores, it was not hard to see why. To be brutally frank, they no longer had a relevant point of view. I couldn't imagine new customers getting excited about the assortments, let alone fashion-conscious customers with large spending budgets.

I gathered together my women's fashion team and asked them about it.

No one seemed to have an answer for this conundrum. But I did.

The point of view that most leapt out to me for Holt Renfrew was that it was a world-class, chic shopping experience. In other words, it was *the* store with its finger on the pulse of cutting-edge fashion. If it wasn't on sale in Holts, it wasn't 'in'. For this to work, we needed a good range of contemporary brands on an exclusive basis. We needed to offer goods to discerning fashionistas that they simply could not buy anywhere else.

Realising this vision was no easy task. Before we could even begin to persuade our intended customer base of our updated point of view, we had to sell it to our would-be suppliers. One contemporary branded clothes company boss even told me straight out: 'We're not sure that Holts is the store for us – it's not chic or fashion forward.' In some cases I had to personally go out and persuade brands to buy into our new point of view. Luckily, after I had signed up a few big names, the others were more inclined to be seen in Holts. They had proof that things were changing.

One of the keys to success was to appoint the fashion director as the person accountable to me for managing the Holt Renfrew point of view. Everything had to be agreed between the merchants and the fashion director.

I've often likened this process of filtering the point of view to sieving flour when you are making a cake. As any half-decent chef will understand, to make the best, melt-in-the-mouth, perfect cake, it is essential to carefully sift the flour to get rid of any unwanted lumps and ensure a little bounce in the mixture. The brands that don't pass the point-of-view test are those lumps. They need to be filtered out and cast aside, or your store will never be relevant.

Once we had populated our fashion floor with a rich mix of the best names in contemporary fashion, we went on to do the same with the menswear floor, updating it with the latest labels. Even though we had worked miracles with the women's brands, we still had to be very persuasive. I recall a very interesting discussion with Leonard Lauder, the chairman of Estée Lauder Corporation. Unfortunately for us, the Lauder fragrance Aramis was already being sold in the 60-plus stores across Canada of our biggest rival, Hudson's Bay. We had very few weapons at our disposal when it came to persuading the owner of this brand to switch to us on an exclusive basis, but this was exactly what we set out to do.

Fortunately, I knew Leonard well and had had many past dealings with his great organisation. We managed to secure a meeting with him in New York to discuss why we should have Aramis exclusively in Canada. To seal the deal, we offered to give the Aramis brand both space and promotional dominance in each of our stores, so it would be a focal point of the men's grooming and cosmetics floor. This would work perfectly for us both. We would get *the* brand, while Lauder would only have one account to service (one of Leonard's main drivers), plus we were a motivated and focused partner.

After some discussion, Leonard gave Holts exclusivity on Aramis: another key plank in establishing our cosmetic point of view.

At the end of that year, Aramis and Holts were delighted with this successful initiative in Canada.

RELEVANT RETAILER *Fortnum & Mason, International*

Five reasons why I believe Fortnum & Mason has a strong point of view:

Quintessentially British brand

Fortnum & Mason, a British brand that is more than three centuries old, makes much of its British roots to deliver its point of view, which is a sense of pleasure. CEO Ewan Venters brilliantly describes the store as 'a diamond being continually polished'. As well as selling its world-famous iconic hampers and vast tea assortment, it works with more than 1000 suppliers throughout the country, from bakers to butchers to chocolatiers. Around 70% of its goods are made in Britain and all are curated towards creating the well-defined point of view of providing pleasure.

Look forwards, not backwards

While Fortnum & Mason celebrates its history, it makes a point of looking forwards, not backwards. By this I mean that

Fortnum & Mason, Piccadilly London – Iconic hamper

it understands and respects its roots, but it does not build strategies or marketing initiatives based on what has gone before. As Ewan Venters often tells his team, if you look in the rear-view mirror too much when driving a car, you will crash.

Stylish store you just have to explore

The layout and presentation in-store nod to the store's heritage and world-class reputation while also embracing the modern, progressive attitude of an evolving speciality store. There is more than a little feeling that you are entering a treasure trove that begs to be explored. It is also kept immaculately: no dust, with smart, clean carpets and mirrors. These 'housekeeping' items may seem incidental, but they make a massive difference to a customer's experience.

Grand window displays

The external windows are beautifully dressed to reflect Fortnum's point of view. In the past, they were dressed by well-known theatre set-designers, and that creativity continues. On my last visit, the windows celebrated Fortnum's fantastic tea heritage. While they were hugely imaginative, they didn't feature one product. They were simply clever visual expressions, using devices such as elephants and tea chests, that nodded to the store's famed expertise in this area. Magnificent.

Connecting with each new generation

Fortnum & Mason actively focuses on energising the brand with each new generation, hosting events in-store and sponsoring food and drink awards. In 2016, Fortnum & Mason published its first-ever cookbook, by Tom Parker Bowles, a young, modern food writer. The beautifully illustrated book includes previously top-secret traditional recipes, as well as Fortnum & Mason's most requested fare, from Welsh rarebit to marmalade tea bread to Scotch eggs.

Once a retailer has defined and understood its point of view, it is crucial to make sure everyone in the organisation understands it too. It may help to articulate it in a brief sentence, so every future decision made at all layers in the store can be weighed against that statement. Thus, everything from merchandise to layout to promotional material can be tested against that point of view to see whether it complements it. If it doesn't, then something has to change.

Let's continue the example of Holts and its international, chic and contemporary point of view to imagine how this approach could play out across the store. The communication and education given to the store team could be as follows:

A point of view

- *What sort of customers do we want to attract?*

Fashion-conscious, cosmopolitan individuals with an interest in new, contemporary styles. Regardless of their age, the Holt Renfrew customer is discerning and body conscious and sets, rather than follows, trends.

- *What kinds of products interest our customers?*

Priorities for our customers are well-edited, cutting-edge fashions and accessories, cosmetics and decorative home furnishings. There is a preference for luxury brands that reflect the latest trends.

- *What adjectives would customers associate with the store?*

Exclusive, stylish, modern, upmarket, indulgent.

- *How do customers feel when they walk into a Holt Renfrew store?*

Excited, pampered and inspired.

- *How is the point of view expressed in the in-store experience?*

The layout is chic and uncluttered, with the spotlight on the designers and their branding. Promotional material is discrete and stylish.

- *How can staff reflect the point of view?*

Front-of-house staff are immaculately turned out in smart, relevant fashions. Customers are offered individual attention and great care is taken at each stage of the purchase, right up until, and including, the final metre, when purchases are brought round to the front of the cash desk and handed to the customer with a smile and a thank you.

Everyone on the team should understand your standards and they should be reinforced in everything you do as a retailer. I always conducted daily, or at the very least weekly, merchandise walk-throughs with my team to ensure every aspect of the store met the agreed point of view. The point of view should be articulated at every internal meeting and it is the job of the retail leadership to make sure everyone is in the habit of testing any suggestion against the point-of-view barometer.

CROWD PLEASER *Waterstones, UK*

It was not that long ago that Waterstones was facing an uncertain future, with many predicting the bookseller would disappear from the high street thanks to stiff competition from Amazon. Now, after years of losses, Waterstones is back in profit and this is all down to a strong point of view. It is firmly targeting book-lovers. Gone are all the offers and promotions. In their place is a superbly curated collection of books displayed in a relaxed, engaging environment that encourages customers to stop and browse. Staff are given the power to choose the books each store stocks, and they are also empowered to write shelf-tag book reviews. If a customer tells them the last book they read, staff know exactly what to recommend next.

It is worth pointing out here that while it is often a deliberate decision from the top to pursue a coherent point of view, it is very often a strategy that is forced upon a company by a particular crisis. In the case of Waterstones, detailed in the Crowd Pleaser section here, the bookstore was facing bankruptcy in 2011. Its new owner, Russian millionaire Alexander Mamut, who had bought it for £53 million, brought in James Daunt, a very experienced MD. Daunt's brief was to turn around the struggling stores. He realised he needed to completely reinvent Waterstones and it is clear that he gave great consideration to its point of view.

A time of crisis is the perfect opportunity to re-examine point of view, just as it is when there is a change of management.

Does this mean that, once the optimum point of view has been decided upon, conveyed and reinforced to the entire organisation, the hard work is all done? The answer is yes and no. But mainly no.

It's fantastic when any retailer clearly defines its point of view, and doing so will make a noticeable difference. However, it's not enough to do it and then continuously filter the brand against the agreed parameters. Everything in business changes all the time, and things change in the world around a retailer too. We all need to change with the times. We've already experienced the marked changes brought about by the internet, technology in general and shifts in consumer attitudes. New competitors are joining the market on an hourly basis. Our economic and political climate looks

A point of view

more uncertain than it has for generations. Who knows what is coming next? Just because your point of view reflects the state of play today, it doesn't necessarily follow that it will be spot on tomorrow, or the next day. In the same way that retailers should regularly test their actions against the filter of their agreed point of view, they should also think in terms of regular analysis of that point of view itself.

One of the hardest aspects of point of view to understand is that it is never truly yours. You, as a retailer, don't *own* that point of view. With a bit of effort, it might be what you intend it to be, but it's not yours. It belongs to your customers. It is their impression of your store and what they have interpreted to be your promise to them. Whether a retailer keeps that promise, and then does so again and again, is up to the retailer. However, it'd be a fool not to.

Mercato Metropolitano, London – Italian market celebrating the joy of fine food

CROWD PLEASER *Mercato Metropolitano, UK*

Mercato Metropolitano is an absolute celebration of the joy of fine food. The Italian market in an old paper market in south London has been designed to replicate food halls in Turin and Milan (it was started by the man behind Eataly – see page 44) and is packed full of regional Italian foods made by artisan producers. The aromas and colours of the superb burrata, or focaccia di Recco, or gnocco fritto, or Neapolitan pizza, or handmade tortellini are utterly intoxicating. There are foods from around the world too, if you fancy branching out. You can eat outside, below the corrugated roof, or shop in a Sicilian supermarket, or even spend a day there in the communal working space. There's a barber, a cookery school, an urban garden and a boxing gym: something for every appetite. If you get a chance, go and explore.

PROFESSIONAL VIEW
How to Be a Relevant Retailer

- The leadership of a retailer must be hardwired into its customers' view or the retailer will fail.
- Costs must be relentlessly reviewed to ensure efficiency and therefore competitiveness.
- The leadership of a retailer must be explicit about the company's unique selling point and continuously invest to extend it.
- Colleague morale is the first step in improving productivity.

Richard Baker
Chairman, Whitbread Plc, International,
and Chairman of the British Retail Consortium, UK

CHAPTER CHECKOUT

✓ All retailers need a point of view. It is a declaration of identity to customers telling them what your stores are all about.

✓ Remember: you don't need *every* customer; you need the *right* customer for you.

✓ Once the point of view is set, everyone in the organisation must buy into it. Every future decision, made at all layers in the store, should be weighed against that point of view, whether the decision concerns merchandise, layout or promotional material.

✓ The CEO, chief merchant and fashion director all need to own the point of view.

✓ Tackle the 'thick middle' stores to ensure you have a consistent point of view throughout the group, remembering that a brand is only as strong as its weakest link.

Chapter four

REINVENTING SHOPPING – THE TECHNOLOGICAL REVOLUTION

Just imagine the following scenario. It is a cold, damp January in London and Amelia is dreaming of her forthcoming holiday in South Africa. No more big jumpers and heavy coats for her: she needs a wardrobe for sun-drenched days on the beach and for balmy evenings hanging out with her friends in nightclubs and bars. Even just five years ago, she'd have headed to London's West End or one of the shopping malls. Now, though, she starts shopping from her sofa.

First up is a video conference with Sara, the personal shopper at Amelia's favourite boutique. Amelia bought two outfits there before Christmas, so Sara understands her style. Sara recommends a number of outfits she'd already picked out and shows them off by superimposing them onto Amelia's avatar. Amelia nods in approval as the avatar spins around, showing off the outfits from all angles. While she's online, Amelia toggles the screen to check out a few customer reviews. Satisfied, she buys one dress online and tells Sara she'll pop into the boutique later to try on some of the other clothes for a final comparison. Later that day, after being greeted by name as she walks into the shop, Amelia goes to the dressing room, which is already stocked with her online selection. Sara has helpfully added some other items, such as a pair of strappy shoes and a handbag. Amelia likes the handbag, so she scans the barcode with her smartphone. She discovers she can get it cheaper at another shop. Sara immediately offers to match the price. Amelia tries on the dress she wasn't quite sure about. It is expensive and a little risqué for her, so she sends a video to three of her closest friends for their opinion. Within seconds the responses come in: three thumbs up. Amelia collects the dress and the handbag, scans a website to check for coupons, saving an additional 10% on the total sale price, and pays using her smartphone. The goods will all be shipped to her home that afternoon.

This scenario is fictional, yet all of the technology is here already. Within two to five years, it will be the norm. Technology represents a huge opportunity for modern retailers and some of the innovations that are appearing in stores all over the world are truly exciting. I just love discovering all these new ways of doing things and then using some of the ideas in my own retail businesses. After all, there is no shame in learning from others' success; the shame is in not doing so. Even after more than 40 years in this industry, I can still say that I am surprised and delighted on a regular basis.

PROFESSIONAL VIEW
How to Be a Relevant Retailer

- The pace of technology-induced disruption in retail is making permanent reinvention the new normal. You have to make sure your organisation is simpler, more agile and capable of testing and learning as it trades the business.
- Unless it is unique, memorable or has an element of surprise, just don't do it.
- Experience rules: it is about creating customer moments that 'wow'. Never has the human and personal touch been so instrumental to differentiate your brand from your competition.

Reinventing shopping – the technological revolution

> • In an era of media and brand saturation, time becomes the most valued currency. Unless it is edited, personalised, relevant to me and rewards my time spent engaging with you as a customer, don't bother me.
>
> *Patrick Bousquet-Chavanne*
> *Executive Director of Customer, Marketing and M&S.com,*
> *Marks & Spencer, International*

Technology is transforming every aspect of the retail business, often at a dizzying rate. Innovations that feel daunting at first quickly become part of normal life. It hardly feels like ten years ago that the first self-service tills appeared. I can still remember the feeling of excitement and curiosity I experienced when I first saw them. Not many of the people who were diligently queuing at the attended cash tills were keen, but I couldn't wait to give them a go.

Admittedly, some people have still not accepted self-service tills. I know too that the robotic reminder to take your change and the brutal bark about unexpected items in the bagging area have become the butts of many a joke. What can't be denied, though, is that countless people now use self-service tills without batting an eyelid. They are symbolic of a sea-change in shopping habits. Technology and the increasing digitisation of the shopping experience have well and truly arrived and are here to stay.

What we are seeing now is only the beginning, too, and the pace of change is breathtaking. As the graphic on page 81 shows, in the late 1980s, the only technology the retail world needed to grapple with was the development of EPOS, or electronic point of sale. These tills were, however, attended. Ecommerce was, of course, a massive leap but the acceleration in new technology since then has been mind-blowing.

It is estimated that digital information already influences around 50% of shop sales, and that number is growing almost exponentially. Not surprisingly, digital retailing has become a category all on its own. In fact, it is so different from what has gone before that it even has its own name: omnichannel retailing. The name indicates that retailers can now interact with customers through a seemingly endless number of channels: websites, physical stores, kiosks, direct mail, call centres, social media, mobile devices, gaming consoles, televisions and home appliances. Retailers that don't keep up with this explosion in the sheer number of ways to shop will be left behind. Relevant retailers are those who manage the feat of integrating all of these disparate channels into one seamless omnichannel experience.

I am constantly on the look-out for what is new and innovative. I have been involved as a member of the advisory board and on the judging panel of the World Retail Congress for a number of years. I do this to keep up to date with all the technological advancements that are happening and to analyse how retailers around the world are ensuring the best in-store customer experiences. It also gives me the opportunity to review the best of the best retail marketing campaigns and to get a firm understanding of how other retailers are ensuring sustainability, who is designing the best web stores and who are the award-winning store architects. Plus, very importantly for me, I can review what the many young, talented retailer entrepreneurs of the year are achieving. This keeps me relevant and up to date. Separately, I have also found that taking my teams to visit new developments at some of the leading technological companies is extremely important.

It is almost impossible to write a chapter on the technology that is so crucial for the omnichannel experience, since much of what I include will be out of date by the time I finish typing it, let alone by the moment you begin reading this book. However, since technology is at the core of so many of the rapid developments today, I would like to explore the areas where it is working successfully now and where it is most likely to come to the fore in the near future.

The following represents a round-up of the key areas in the omnichannel experience:

Experience enhancement

In this new era of retailing, visiting a physical store today and in the future must be exciting, magnetic, entertaining and engaging. Customers should look upon a store visit with the same level of excitement and anticipation that they would a visit to the cinema or going out for a meal with friends – in short, as a feeling and experience that simply can't be replicated online.

Digital technology can brighten up previously static or lifeless store windows. Vibrant interactive screens can be programmed to show a constantly changing display that reacts to influences such as the weather.

how quickly is **the retail world changing?**

1995 - invest in a 5-year plan, spend $50m on a new system, minimal failure risk

2015 - full agility, constant short-term planning, low-cost high-frequency developments

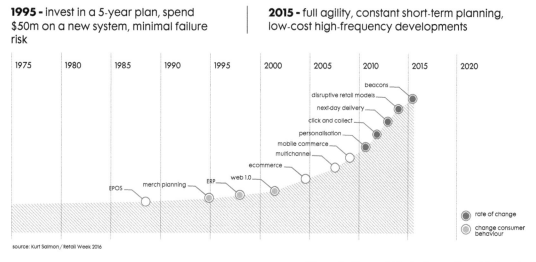

source: Kurt Salmon / Retail Week 2016

Figure 1. How quickly is the retail world changing?

Touch-screen technology can allow customers to assemble outfits, design products or even place orders when the store is closed.

Bloomingdale's Manhattan flagship ran a Father's Day promotion in 2015 in which it encouraged passers-by to interact with its digital windows via touch screens that showed its range. If they liked what they saw, they could text 'POLO' for a link to a checkout page. They could even opt to have their options hand-delivered to the sidewalk outside – completing the entire impulse buy without ever entering the store.

Burberry's flagship store in London's Regent Street features huge screens throughout the entire perimeter of the interior. This digital wall pulsates with content, featuring everything from runway feeds to audiovisual content, mirrors and adverts. Other smaller digital displays are propped up against staircases and clothes racks. Theatrically, the scenes on the screens constantly change, displaying mini-dramas such as a thunderstorm that drenches customers in a virtual downpour. Speakers add to the drama, playing the sound of a rainstorm complete with a clap of thunder.

CROWD PLEASER *Samsung, International*

Technology retailer Samsung's flagship New York store, Samsung 837, is so high tech it doesn't even sell anything (unless you count the in-store café). At the heart of the 55,000-square-foot, three-storey building is a massive cinema screen that shows everything from live streams of product announcements to the Oscars. Guests in the 75-seat theatre can take advantage of the 'selfie station' and have their face beamed onto the giant screen just long enough to Instagram it. Elsewhere there is a space for technology-based art installations, a virtual reality tunnel, 4D chairs and a playroom. Samsung describes the store as a 'physical manifestation of the company's brand'.

A successful omnichannel digital strategy does not simply offer a seamless shopping experience, although this is vital. It should aim to deliver a revolution in customer experiences and expectations of the sort that only comes along every 50 years or so. This is a big challenge, but, as I have shown here, plenty of retailers are meeting it.

Virtual and augmented reality

It has been predicted that virtual and augmented reality will reshape retail. The technology gives customers the opportunity to try on clothes without ever having to visit a physical store or, when they are in-store, the freedom to 'see' things in the virtual world, such as what furniture would look like in their homes. It really does seem like the ultimate personalised experience and is undeniably very exciting indeed.

Firstly, though, for the uninitiated, the basics. Virtual reality (VR) immerses the customer in a simulated world and requires standalone technologies such as headsets and hand controllers. Augmented reality (AR) involves overlaying virtual elements onto the real world as seen through devices such as smartphones or tablets.

Marks & Spencer UK chose VR to launch its new homewares range in autumn 2015. Customers put on a VR headset and, using Oculus Rift and Leap Motion technology, could select items from the LOFT range to create their ideal living space. French retailer Leroy Merlin also makes use of Oculus Rift to enable customers to view its entire catalogue of ready-built kitchens virtually. Across the Atlantic, American home-improvement chain Lowe's has gone one step further and installed spaces in 19 of its stores that allow customers to see a 3D mock-up of their own renovation project. Called Holoroom, the simulated space can be personalised with individual room sizes, equipment, colours and finishings. Customers can use Lowe's headsets in-store or take home a free Google Cardboard viewer (available in on-site vending machines). If this all sounds expensive, think of the upside: if customers get a holistic, or immersive, view of how certain looks can completely change their room at home, it is far more likely that they will stick with the retailer that enabled them to have this vision.

There are numerous creative uses of AR too. Shiseido's AR make-up mirror takes an image of a customer's face so the sales assistant can show them what various shades of make-up will look like. IKEA has an AR catalogue to help customers visualise how certain items of furniture will look in their homes. The app also measures the size of the products against the surrounding room and fixtures to offer as realistic a size as possible. Lacoste uses AR to enable customers to quickly 'try on' its entire product range in-store and view the results in 3D. Customers can also take photos to send to their friends via Facebook, Twitter or email.

While the use of VR and AR is still in the early stages, it is widely seen to have huge potential. The industry is already predicting that annual revenues will grow from $1 billion to $30 billion by 2020[10]. In time, as VR in particular becomes more mainstream and customers buy their own headsets, more so-called v-commerce will move back into the home. Customers will be able to walk through stores and try on clothes without leaving their sofa. The trick for physical retailers is to find new ways for VR and AR to remain relevant in-store.

---

10   Digi-Capital. Augmented/Virtual Reality Report 2017

RELEVANT RETAILER *Lego, International*

Five ways that Lego has energised its stores using technology:

Constantly evolving

The company has a saying: the word 'technology' only applies to things that occur after you were born. Tablets and smartphones are not technology for children born today – they are just part of the world they've been born into. In the future, AR and VR will just be part of that world too. To remain relevant, the technology environment in-store needs to constantly evolve.

Stores are more than just bricks and mortar

At a time when increasing numbers of people are buying toys online, Lego is revamping its store network because it sees its physical stores as a crucial part of its offering. They give its customers the chance to completely immerse themselves in the models and to see and experience constructions first hand.

Physical play meets digital

The stores offer an enticing mix of giant Lego constructions that children can climb inside (everything from full-sized trains to telephone boxes) and interactive digital play areas.

Interactive

Lego introduced augmented reality in-store kiosks in 2010. Customers could hold up boxes of Lego sets in front of the 'digital box' screen and the finished item would appear on top of the box on the screen. In 2015, it released another app, called Lego X, which uses networked Lego bricks to create a 3D model. The bricks are sensor and gyroscope enabled, which allows kids to see a real-time depiction of their models as they design them.

Personalisation

Lego's new flagship store in London's Leicester Square (opened in 2016) has a unique Mosaic Portrait system. Kids can have their photos taken in a booth, and the photos are then automatically turned into mosaic models of their face. The end result is presented to the customer in a box, so they can make their own portrait out of Lego bricks.

Lego Flagship, London

Dressing rooms

The purpose of in-store technology is to add value or utility for the consumer, not just to be there for the sake of it. It can come into its own in one particular area where the user experience has long been neglected: dressing rooms. The days of hanging around in half-naked desperation, hoping against hope a shop assistant will come to your aid, are now, thankfully, moving behind us.

A number of retailers, including Ralph Lauren, have launched smart dressing-room mirrors. Radio-frequency identification technology is used to recognise the items a customer has bought in with them and render the products on screen. Mirrors show other available colours and sizes, as well as recommended products based on the style chosen. A 'call an associate' button connects to a sales person's tablet to call them to the dressing room. There is also an option for customers to log into their online account and add items to their wish list. Customers can then sign up to receive alerts when the item is reduced or included in a promotion.

Luxury designer Rebecca Minkoff has 'magic mirrors' in her stores that allow customers to change the light settings. It is a well-known fact that clothing looks different under differing lighting conditions. This technology allows the person in the dressing room to check the look in conditions such as night-time and daylight.

Many customers find self-scrutiny in shop changing rooms dispiriting, possibly because more than a third of people in the UK (for example) are unhappy with their body image. Smart mirrors are set to play a role in combating this by delivering personalised compliments to customers. Home furnishing giant IKEA has introduced a motivational mirror that uses motion sensor technology to detect a customer's facial and body features before activating a correspondingly appropriate compliment.

Magic mirrors can even take away the need for customers to undress at all. Topshop uses mirrors that incorporate built-in cameras that track the customer's body and reflect it on screen. Augmented reality then superimposes selected items of clothing onto the customer's reflection.

PROFESSIONAL VIEW
How to Be a Relevant Retailer

Prioritise the following:
- the quality and enthusiasm of the people;
- the speed at which the business is enabled to move;
- the customer-centric nature of decisions and strategy;
- the sustainable nature of the business model in an ever-changing and disruptive environment.

Bernie Brookes
CEO and MD, Edcon, South Africa

Personalised experiences

Ecommerce is perfectly suited to providing customers with a personalised online experience. Physical stores are increasingly catching up now too, thanks to digital technology. The aim of the game is to pinpoint exactly what a customer would like to purchase, even if they do not know such a product exists before they enter a store.

Uniqlo has a unique take on the endeavour with its UMood sales tool, which it claims can match a customer with a product by reading the customer's mind. First launched in Sydney, Australia, UMood is a standalone unit that looks a little like a large gaming machine. Customers sit in a chair facing a large screen and are asked to wear a headset with a forehead sensor. They watch short films of just a few seconds featuring such things as a woman reading in a forest, a stormy day in the city, a man standing on top of a mountain, a kitten, and a man dancing. Using information from five data points, which are interest, like, concentration, stress and drowsiness, UMood presents four alternative t-shirts and measures the customer's response, before announcing the 'perfect' one to suit that individual's mood. Even if the neurological theory behind the idea is not 100% credible, it is an interesting way to help narrow the choice for customers and personalise their shopping experience.

Another imaginative use of personalisation comes from the French shopping centre Klépierre, with its Inspiration Corridor. This is a booth that uses facial and body recognition, as well as an individual's purchasing history, to make personalised shopping recommendations.

One of the most significant moves forward in personally engaging customers is via beacons. Beacons are small, low-cost, battery-operated wireless devices that transmit a weak signal to other Bluetooth-enabled devices close by. They reach out to customers when they walk past and instantly create a more engaging in-store experience. They might offer rewards, discounts, recommendations and deals. The goal is to create a deeper personal relationship with a tailored experience. Individual customers are encouraged to feel the effort they made to visit the store is both justified and valued.

They can be used for regular offers or specific campaigns. Meadowhall Shopping Centre in Sheffield, UK, used beacons to enhance its ladies' night promotions. Customers had to download the app and then were offered freebies, discounts and prizes at retailers such as Hotel Chocolat, Krispy

Kreme, Cath Kidston and House of Fraser, after receiving notifications every time they got close to a beacon.

The majority of retailers on London's Regent Street, from Hamley's to Armani to Hackett, deploy beacons to push exclusive and personalised marketing messages to customers. People shopping in the area receive alerts and tailored content about everything from in-store promotions to exclusive offers as they pass stores. The app also encourages shoppers to anonymously input their preferences. This, in turn, helps retailers to build a more detailed profile of customers who redeem online special offers, respond to mobile adverts and go on to enter physical stores.

There are numerous other applications for beacons too. They have also been successfully trialled in click and collect. When a click-and-collect customer reaches a certain radius of the store, a notification is sent to the pickers and prompts staff to begin assembling the order. Some chains have used them as sensors to track customer journeys and analyse dwell time in particular aisles. Another development in beacon technology is an alert for shoppers in a physical store that an item previously placed in the basket of the online equivalent retailer is in stock and ready to buy and take home right now.

PROFESSIONAL VIEW
How to Be a Relevant Retailer

- Be much more customer centric. Retailers are generally sales centric. There's a big difference.
- Technology makes unique, well-chosen product all the more important.
- Stop thinking channel, or even multichannel. Think convenience and accessibility.
- Space: most retailers need (a lot) less, but of better quality and location.

Charlie Mayfield
Chairman, John Lewis Partnership, International

John Lewis, Leeds UK – Reaching for the sky

Reducing friction

Streamlining the process and reducing friction are key to a seamless omnichannel shopping experience. The term 'friction-free shopping' describes how each element of the journey becomes simpler and more intuitive, making it easier to begin and complete the purchase. Smooth and convenient transactions are the order of the day. This has long been the core of Amazon's business strategy and why it has been a success: everything is so easy to buy. Fill your virtual basket, click and then a little while later it all just shows up on your doorstep.

It is a real priority for physical shops to identify bottlenecks, or friction points, that might hinder shoppers from quickly and easily finding and buying the products they want. It is here that technology can come into its own.

CROWD PLEASER *Alibaba, International*

The Chinese fashion market is fast becoming a global force, thanks to the increasing wealth of its middle classes, the growth of global shopping and the increase in global consumption. Alibaba leads the market in China, with an 8% share in 2016, but globally it is the second largest internet retailer, with a 14% share. If you don't know it now, you soon will. As well as fashion, it sells everything from heavy machinery to consumer electronics. Its ecommerce strategy, pioneered by founder Jack Ma (who is already being favourably compared to the likes of Jeff Bezos and Steve Jobs), is based on the 'iron triangle', which focuses on commerce, logistics and finance. In terms of commerce, the retailer operates on eight platforms, including Alibaba.com, Tmall.com, Taobao.com and AliExpress.com. Logistics encompasses the network of information and delivery systems that efficiently and quickly moves goods to where they need to be. Just like Amazon, Alibaba controls every stage of the purchase and delivery process. Meanwhile, finance makes paying for those goods safe and convenient. Indeed, Alipay, the company's secure online payment system, has become ubiquitous beyond Alibaba's platforms.

Reinventing shopping – the technological revolution

One of the biggest disconnects between online and physical channels is product range and availability. Quite simply, it is a lot easier online to display a range that is almost infinite and certainly far larger than can be crammed into the confines of a bricks-and-mortar environment. In-store kiosks can go a long way towards addressing this. Debenhams, M&S and many other stores have kiosks installed in every store in the UK and they are very successful. They allow customers a convenient way to browse, order and pay for items that are not in stock at that particular store. A variation on this theme that is also picking up speed across the globe is for shop assistants to carry tablets to check item availability. Systems can be set up to track inventory across multiple channels, showing the retailer what stock is available and where it is, making it easy to locate items customers are asking for. Fashion retailer Oasis (UK) offers this service across its platforms, via 'Seek and Send'. Store assistants can order items on behalf of customers who can't find what they are looking for. On top of this, there is a similar service on the retailer's website. When an item is not available online, Oasis will endeavour to track it down in its bricks-and-mortar stores before dispatching it directly to the customer.

Retailers can also make great use of technology behind the scenes to smooth the omnichannel shopping experience. Predictive analytics helps shops to understand and anticipate the needs and behaviours of shoppers. Advances in this area will empower retailers to predict peak times in store traffic so they can make sure enough store assistants are available, maintain stock levels and anticipate buyer behaviour. Better predictions mean a better experience in-store.

RETAIL GRAVEYARD *Clinton Cards, UK*

Five reasons why failure to recognise changes in technology led to the retailer's bankruptcy in 2012:

Hubris

At its peak (having bought its main rival card chain, Birthdays, in 2004), Clinton Cards controlled 25% of the UK greetings card market and owned 1,145 shops, making it one of the UK's largest retail chains. After being dominant for so long, it was slow to notice younger, leaner rivals gaining ground. The Lewin family, which founded the chain, liked to say that their industry was watertight because the desire to send cards ('sentiment') would never go out of fashion. While they might be right, they failed to see that we would change the way we buy cards.

Dismissive of digital

The first e-cards appeared as long ago as 1994, but it took a while for them to reach the sophistication we know today. Even so, Clinton Cards was dismissive of the potential popularity of digital cards, appearing to be sure that customers would still prefer to make a special trip to the high street to buy greetings cards.

Late to innovate

Clinton Cards launched an ecommerce site in April 2000 that offered a limited service allowing customers to personalise cards and set reminders for special dates. Coincidentally, rival Moonpig launched in the same year and within seven years had secured 90% of the online greetings card market, with nearly 6 million cards shipped.

No marketing effort

Part of the problem behind Clinton Cards' e-card service was a failure to promote it. While the products were on offer, the retailer didn't make anything like the noise of rivals such as Moonpig and Funky Pigeon (which was bought by rival WH Smith in 2010). There was no obvious attempt to make a cohesive omnichannel experience either.

Emphasis on bricks and mortar

Clinton Cards' business model of plastering the high street with an increasing number of stores proved to be catastrophically out of date. Its rental bill was £80 million a year when it went into administration, at a time when a lot of the card business had already migrated online.

Payment and checkout options

The days of cash have long been numbered. It is now the norm to queue up at a till and pay with a tap or swipe of our credit or debit cards, or go to a self-service checkout, scan our goods and do the same. Even so, however they end up paying, no one likes to queue. Indeed, one of the main obstacles that deter shoppers from visiting physical stores is the fact they will almost always have to queue to pay. But, the end is in sight! Before long, the days of queues will disappear and be forgotten, just like cash.

Many stores are already experimenting with throwing out the cash till altogether. Retailers such as Burberry and Apple have added a layer of convenience by bringing sales staff out from behind tills. The assistants have mobile points of sale and personally guide customers through the purchase process, eliminating queues and adding a new layer of personalisation.

There are new developments, such as MishiPay, that allow customers to pick up products, scan the barcode with their phone, pay with their phone and then simply leave the shop with their purchase without having to wait to connect with a sales assistant. The shopper can also opt to have the product in question delivered straight to their home.

We are already seeing a growing trend for retailers to allow people to order ahead and pay, so staff can begin preparing items for collection in advance of their visit. Expect to see a lot more about 'buy online and pick up in-store' (BOLPUIS). Starbucks' Mobile Order & Pay app is currently taking 5 million transactions per month. Within just three months of launch, 20% of the retailer's mobile transactions were conducted in this way. Taco Bell says that its customers spend 17% more per transaction using BOLPUIS. It is very easy to click 'yes' to the question 'Do you want to add a side of beans to the order?' online. Ordering ahead encourages impulse buying.

Another innovative development, which encourages repeat business, is mobile payment apps that mimic ecommerce transactions in bricks-and-mortar stores. Supermarket giant Walmart has a mobile payments app that links to product codes and automatically triggers coupons, promotions and savings that are then received at checkout. The customer doesn't even need to swipe each product, as the system detects them while they're still in the customer's basket. Their phone can be left in their pocket or handbag once they have checked in via the app.

It should be noted that the growth in mobile payments has been one of the most significant developments for the fashion industry in China – a huge and growing business. WeChat has over 800 million monthly active users, and 200 million users of the platform have linked payment cards with their WeChat accounts[11]. Some 34% of users spend over 500 RMB (approximately $72) per month via WeChat, which is six times the amount of the previous year. There is a huge trend towards mobile payments replacing the Chinese wallet.

The opportunities for digital technology in the physical store environment are just as boundless as in the online one, perhaps even more so for experience-seeking customers. Plus, used well, they can link the various platforms and create a superior omnichannel experience.

Relevant retailers need to be imaginative and up to date with what is available so that they can adopt these innovations ahead of the trend. Being three years behind the curve will not create a buzz. Inevitably, if you experiment with new technology, not everything will take off. In some cases the effects will be hard to quantify. This is not a reason to avoid getting stuck in.

---

11   WeChat, *Data Report*, 2016

CHAPTER CHECKOUT

✓ Technology is transforming every aspect of the retail business and the pace of change is breathtaking. Technology has a key role to play in experiences that customers now crave.

✓ Use technology creatively to enhance every aspect of the shopping experience, from the dressing room to the checkout process.

✓ Ensure you have allocated sufficient travel budgets to benchmark the best of the best in innovations.

✓ Attend technology conferences and supplier demonstrations where you can to remain 100% relevant.

✓ You can't always be the best in all areas of technology; it's unaffordable. I have always believed it better to invest in specific areas where you need to win in order to be relevant.

Chapter five

SUPPLY CHAIN REVOLUTION

For decades, the supply chain was seen to be the somewhat unglamorous side of retail. If people thought about it at all, they dismissed it as warehousing and 'to do with moving boxes of merchandise from here to there and from there to here'. While store management had to accept that the supply chain is a necessity and a fact of retail life, acceptance was frequently grudging. It is clearly a cost and easy to dismiss as a drain on already wafer-thin margins. The only people really interested in logistics were supply chain practitioners, whose responsibility it was to keep stores fully stocked. As long as the shelves were kept full, no one else really bothered to get too involved unless something went wrong – and then everyone in the business was suddenly a supply chain expert.

Reflecting on progress over the past 25 years of my retail career, I clearly recall introducing the first central distribution centre for House of Fraser in 1995. In the process, we moved the organisation from direct-store delivery (20–30 trucks lining up in the loading bays of every store during peak times) to a slick, centralised process. It was a cumbersome mission, to put it mildly, but the transformation to a modern, mechanised and efficient distribution centre instantly paid dividends.

Over the past few years a lot has changed. There has been a quiet revolution, moving from a process where suppliers deliver directly to a store's back doors to centralised distribution and now to a virtual stock process.

Today, thanks to the digital revolution and the rapid succession of astonishing innovations introduced by a handful of retailers, getting merchandise direct to the consumer, in the shortest, most convenient way possible, is a significant competitive advantage. Supply chain logistics is, if not 'sexy', certainly at the top of every retailer's mind. After all, any retailer who cannot get the right product to the right customer at the right time is going to become irrelevant very quickly in the hyper-pressurised world of retail in which we live today.

To understand how important this is all the way down the line, consider the following scenario. Imagine you are a customer about to buy a Dyson vacuum cleaner. There are, today, multiple outlets that sell Dysons, from department stores to high street electrical shops to online home stores. The chances are, the selling price of the machine you want will be pretty much the same wherever you buy it from. There is, after all, only so much discount any outlet can give. Prices can only be eroded so far before profit becomes non-existent. So, how do retailers differentiate themselves today? What will influence your decision as to where to buy your brand new Dyson?

The answer lies in how the various retail chains deliver the goods. Variables such as how quickly the customer can get their hands on the item, the availability of home delivery, and the cost and speed of home delivery all make a difference. There are dozens of different variables on offer today, and rest assured that customers will be weighing them up to find the one that best suits their lifestyle. A cost-conscious consumer might, for example, consider the relative merits of paying delivery costs versus the need to stay at home on a workday to sign for their vacuum cleaner. The cost of parking near the high street or shopping mall in order to pick one up themselves will also come into play. To another customer, time might be of the essence, so they'll head to a shop that promises same-day delivery. If convenience is a factor, the customer might be swayed by a shop that offers click and collect.

In short: a crucial new battleground for relevant retailers is all about the supply chain. Getting this right in a world where instant gratification is the norm offers a substantial competitive advantage.

PROFESSIONAL VIEW
How to Be a Relevant Retailer

- Service must be delivered by highly trained personnel.
- Develop your merchandise mix – maintain inventories that are current, pertinent and wanted by the consumer with an emphasis on appropriate balance. Having merchandise readily available in the store, or online, is imperative.
- Retailers have become distracted by technology, gathering increasing amounts of data that in many cases is either not relevant or not important, and in many cases is not used at all.
- Balance the opportunities between bricks and mortar and the internet, making both quality endeavours.
- Retailers must create a shopping experience for the customer and extend themselves to make shopping more fun and more interesting.

Burt Tansky
Vice Chairman, TRAUB, International, and
former CEO and Chairman, Neiman Marcus, USA

Let me share a recent personal experience to show how powerful a well-run supply chain can be. Not long ago, my wife Karen and I decided that we would supplement our healthy diet by finally succumbing to the juicer craze. She carefully researched and pinpointed the appliance that would be just perfect for our needs. We agreed we wanted to go to a physical store because, while the specifications looked spot on, we both felt we'd like to see it in the flesh before finally committing to the chosen model. The juicer in question was on sale at a central London department store.

The juicer turned out to be fit for purpose. I told the assistant that we'd take one right away. It was then that we discovered to our dismay that it was out of stock.

'We can order one for you,' she said helpfully. 'It will be here early next week.'

Feeling a little put out, we refused the offer and exited the store onto the busy street outside. Taking out my smartphone, I typed in some details and discovered that the juicer was sold in John Lewis, just down the road.

Unbelievably, when we arrived, the juicer was sold out. The very helpful John Lewis partner in charge of kitchen gadgets explained that we could purchase one online and it would be delivered on Monday. He also offered a click-and-collect option.

'Could you deliver it to Waitrose?' I enquired. 'We have one just 100 metres from our home.'

'Of course,' said the partner with a smile. 'We can get you one there tomorrow, by 12 noon.'

And there you have it in a nutshell. A smooth supply chain solves a customer's problem at a stroke, delivering the product they want, when they want it, with a minimum amount of fuss.

To understand the potential, it might help to go back to basics: What does the supply chain involve? The supply chain consists of everything from the time the product is first manufactured to shipping it, distribution and finally getting it into the customer's hands. This is why it is sometimes also known as 'end-to-end'. While often fiendishly complex to organise, these are all basic, fundamental aspects of a retail operation. They are also a significant cost to the business, in terms of transport, human resources and storage facilities.

In each of the retail businesses I have led, I have spent much time reducing supply chain costs by becoming more efficient. In crude terms, this meant bringing down the number of times a product is touched, whether by cutting down on the frequency with which it is moved from one factory to another or reducing the number of kilometres it covers on its journey (land and/or sea). Efforts can also be made to reduce the number of shipments to a single destination by grouping products together. Thus, if a retailer buys adult t-shirts from one supplier, it makes sense for everyone for the shop to accept deliveries for children's t-shirts from that same supplier, at the same time.

One area that always receives particular attention in the bid to cut costs is the amount of physical space that is required to store product, pick it and get it out for delivery. At one time, most retailers were completely reliant on giant warehouses to store their products. These warehouses, often of a million or more square feet, were filled with floor-to-ceiling racking. A fleet of forklifts and skilled forklift handlers would be deployed to sweep up and down the aisles between the racks, manoeuvring pallets of goods up and down the racks.

Advances in automation and capacity, such as mechanised racking, driverless vehicles, GPS tracking and laser guidance, have transformed this process. It is now possible to have a matrix of racking with no permanent aisles at all.

More advanced warehouse systems represent a huge cost reduction for the retailer, Since there is less need for numerous aisles, there is no aisle wastage and a reduced need for space. As a consequence, warehouses have shrunk in size considerably and this represents a massive cost saving. Additionally, skilled forklift operators are no longer required. These are all efficiency and productivity gains that help make a business profitable.

Of course, while cost reductions are important to running a successful business, they are not always about *saving* the retailer money. As I have said here on so many occasions already, relevance is about enhancing the *customer experience*.

CROWD PLEASER *Starship Technologies, USA*

A small box on wheels dubbed 'Robochops' is currently on trial, delivering takeaways in Greenwich, New York. The six-wheeled cube has a combination locked lid and enough space inside for a food-delivery bag. It is essentially a mobile locker that makes its own way to a customer's house to deliver their food. It averages four miles per hour (with a top speed of ten miles per hour) and will stop when it comes within two yards of a human. A GPS system prevents it from driving off the kerb into oncoming traffic and alarms controlled by robot handlers based in Estonia are used to prevent theft or interference. A taste of things to come.

It is a constant challenge to keep up. At one point, many retailers believed getting the supply chain right simply boiled down to getting their online operation up to speed and sorting out an effective home delivery service, perhaps in partnership with a courier. This might have kept retailers in the 'me too' brigade for a brief window of time, but consumers' expectations quickly moved on. Indeed, research from high street and online retailer Next is quite telling. In 2010, 95% of this retailer's online orders were placed via desktop computer. Just five years on, that figure had shrunk to 37%, with customers turning to mobile devices, tablets and a plethora of other ordering mechanisms. Similarly, in 2010, 87% of all Next orders were delivered to a customer's home address. By 2015, less than half (45%) were going to stores for pick-up. Customers do not want to choose between online ordering, home delivery and purchasing in-store. Today they want to choose between any number of ways to purchase and receive the goods so that they can do so in the way they want.

It is not a static situation either. With this constant stream of better and more convenient ways to receive goods, customer expectations are only ever going to increase. Over the next decade, consumers will stretch supply chains to their limits, demanding that their purchases are placed in their hands wherever they may be. After all, we already take it for granted that when we push a button we get a taxi right where we are, almost immediately. It's the norm now that when we turn on the TV, we can watch exactly what we want, when we want, rather than waiting patiently for the TV schedule. It's the same with the service we get from retail, whether online or on the high street. Customers already 'get' next-day delivery, click and collect, and kiosks, but what are retailers going to do next to make customers' time-poor lives even more pleasant and convenient?

A key driver of advances in supply chain logistics is the quest to improve the way the consumer receives their goods. While many retailers have made clever improvements to this field, there has been one that has, without a doubt, led the way in many of the developments that have transformed supply chains: Amazon. Indeed, arguably, supply chain management has been the key to Amazon's success, transforming the company from a lowly online bookseller launched in 1995 to the world's most formidable and dominant retailer.

CROWD PLEASER *Amazon, International*

In the pursuit of faster delivery, lower costs and greater market share, Amazon invests all of its free cash flow into growth initiatives and pioneering approaches to doing business. To understand just how much of a trendsetter it has been, look at some of its achievements:

- *As early as 1997, Amazon launched its 1-Click ordering process, which enables customers to make online purchases with a single click. In 2013, this evolved into 'anticipatory shopping'. Amazon has patented a predictive algorithm that starts boxing and moving products before the customer clicks the 'buy' button.*

- *Amazon Prime launched in 2005, as an annual membership that offered free two-day shipping on thousands of items. Over time, this changed into next-day delivery. Now, just as many retailers have caught up and are themselves offering free shipping, Amazon has taken this a step further and is offering one-hour deliveries with Amazon Prime Now (launched in December 2014).*

- *Amazon CEO Jeff Bezos announced in 2013 that the retailer was developing a drone-based delivery system, Amazon Prime Air. Customers who order packages that weigh less than five pounds and who live within 10 miles of an Amazon Fulfilment Centre will receive their orders within 30 minutes or less. While there are some regulatory hurdles to overcome, these drones could be delivering a package near you very soon.*

- *In warehousing, Amazon has continued to expand the parameters on what it is possible to do. In 2012, the retailer bought Kiva Systems, a provider of robotic and automated warehouse solutions. In 2015, it was rebranded Amazon Robotics, and its warehouses now run a complex system of automated robots that can pick, pack and sort shipments, all without the need of any human assistance whatsoever.*

While the innovations listed in the Crowd Pleaser section above have helped Amazon to keep ahead of the competition when they were first introduced, they are now a ticket-to-play for anyone who wants to remain relevant. Amazon is, without a doubt, the master of customer-friendly logistics. When a customer buys a product from Amazon, it is almost guaranteed that they will get it in the allotted time and be kept informed along the way with delivery tracking, whether the product will be delivered overnight or a week from today. Amazon is not alone, though, and there have been impressive innovations from other key UK retailers, such as Tesco, John Lewis and Argos (see my thoughts on Argos in the Relevant Retailer section below). Tesco has focused on radio-frequency identification (RFID), which has been around in retail since the turn of the millennium. RFID is integral to its F&F clothing range, giving the retailer a more accurate, real-time view of its inventory at all times. Tesco is now working on ways to harness the data to create a more predictive model so it can react more quickly to customer demands.

Department store group John Lewis is constantly looking at improvements in its supply chain logistics. Each November and December, it introduces a training academy to assist the 700 temporary workers who join its core online workforce of 200 to ensure the festive season goes smoothly. All part-time workers are compelled to graduate from this programme before being able to pick and pack orders, to ensure the highest levels of order accuracy are maintained. This ensures consistency in the John Lewis customer experience.

RELEVANT RETAILER *Argos, UK*

Five ways Argos has succeeded with supply chain innovations:

Click-and-collect pioneer

In 2001, Argos was the first retailer to launch click and collect. Observers were initially sceptical, but a quarter of all online sales now culminate in this service.[12] Customers appreciate the speed, convenience, value and lack of delivery fees of this option.

Early adopter of same-day delivery

In 2010, Argos began working with the Shutl courier service and was able to offer same-day delivery in as little as 90 minutes from certain Argos stores.

---

12   Barclays. Click and Collect Report, August 2016

Nationwide same day

Argos has now recruited its own fleet of more than 3,300 new drivers, who are based at the company's stores. This enables the chain to offer its Fast Track home delivery service, providing customers across the UK with same-day deliveries up to 10pm, on items that can be ordered as late as 6pm. Many other chains offer one-hour delivery in the southeast, but introducing the service nationwide is another game-changer.

Fast Track collection

Fast Track collection is also on offer. Customers who pre-pay online can collect their goods at the in-store collection counters within 60 seconds of being served.

On track with Underground shopping

Argos was the first retailer to team up with London Underground to launch an 'Argos Collect' store at Cannon Street Tube station. The millions of London Underground customers can use their smartphones during their journey and choose from 20,000 products that can be collected from the station. Small digital concessions have also been opened in branches of Homebase and Sainsbury's.

Amazon, Tesco, Argos et al. all have a similar starting point: they begin with the customer and work backwards. As we have seen, the modern consumer is demanding and tech savvy. They know what they want, they know how they want to get it and they know the price they are prepared to pay. This means understanding their preferences and offering a great experience that includes a wide selection, competitive pricing, a convenient purchasing process and reliable product delivery.

CROWD PLEASER *Parcelly, UK*

Parcelly capitalises on click and collect, one of the fastest-growing categories in the supply chain logistics sector, and seeks to tackle the so-called last-mile delivery problem. Rather than requiring them to pick from a list of existing collection locations, Parcelly allows customers to request locations where they'd like to collect their goods. Local shops and business owners are invited to partner with Parcelly to build the number of locations on offer. It could be the local garage, a department store or a food business – these are all opportunities for retailers to increase footfall.

From the customer's point of view, it is all pretty straightforward. It is as easy as paying for their goods online or at the till and checking an app that confirms delivery is on the way (which may be to home, work or a friend's house), or even collecting the goods from a purpose-designed locker in a public facility. For the retailer, though, this is the toughest challenge yet to get right. Deliveries have to be planned meticulously, travelling many miles, often through highly congested areas, yet somehow arrive within a very narrow time window, or possibly at a precisely specified time.

Retailers have to constantly adapt in the face of perpetually evolving expectations. If you are in any doubt about the power of the consumer, consider the first thing you do when a retailer doesn't deliver, literally or metaphorically. You complain to your friends and family. Except this won't just be a grumble at the dinner table or down at the pub. This will most likely be a very public ticking off for the retailer concerned via a social media post that might be seen by dozens, even hundreds and thousands. One survey found that 12% take to platforms such as Twitter or Facebook to escalate gripes with retailers.[13] Why bother to spend time penning an angry letter or dialling a call centre when it is possible to let off steam within seconds to express irritation at a shop's poor service? The customer in question may feel better after they have done so and then quickly forget about it, but the effects of such complaints can do lasting damage to the image of a retailer, particularly if a number of people express disquiet.

---

13   Institute of Customer Service, Survey, May 2015

Supply chain revolution

If a retailer makes a delivery promise, they have to stick to it.

RETAIL GRAVEYARD *Webvan, USA*

Five reasons why online grocer Webvan's supply chain led to its collapse:

Over-ambitious launch

Webvan launched in 1999 with the promise of cheap groceries and 30-minute delivery windows, saying it would completely redefine how Americans bought their food and drink. Millions of dollars were invested in an aggressive growth strategy that centred on the home-delivery supply-chain model.

Supply exceeded demand

At over 350,000 square feet and costing $25–30 million to build, each distribution centre was capable of fulfilling 8000 customer orders per day and could hold up to 50,000 stock-keeping units (SKUs). In reality, each warehouse stocked just 20,000 SKUs and received just over 2000 orders per day.

Supply chain strategy did not align with market

Although excessive capacity was costing Webvan millions, it failed to respond. In fact, it went on opening its giant distribution centres in every new state it expanded into.

Higher costs

Webvan's costs were far higher than traditional supermarket supply chains, in an industry where margins are as little as 1–1.5%. Yet, its business model required the additional expense of Webvan employees picking items for orders, as opposed to customers collecting them themselves in a bricks-and-mortar environment.

Poor pricing structure

To make matters worse, Webvan marketed itself as having prices 5% lower than conventional stores. The intention was that volumes would be high enough to offset the losses of the supply chain. They weren't. Webvan closed in 2001, having lost millions of dollars.

So, what does a modern retailer need to do to remain relevant in terms of supply chain logistics? What will be the key drivers in the future?

Without question, delivering on your promise will continue to be crucial. The focus will be on flawless execution. Retailers need to have enough product in stock, which means keeping accurate and detailed demand forecasts, and they need to get it to customers in the way they want.

Speed of delivery will be a primary concern. This means that retailers will have to give careful consideration to the number of delivery hubs and warehouses they run. There is little point in having one (albeit highly automated) depot in South West England when customers all over the UK demand next-day, or even same-day, delivery. The future undoubtedly lies in multiple distribution hubs, which ensure goods can be delivered to customers in a narrow window of time. Retailers may need to get inventive and use their physical stores more like mini-warehouses from which online orders can be locally fulfilled. While a full catalogue of product needs to be available in whichever distribution centre they use, the trick is also going to lie in accurate forecasting, since too much, or too little, inventory can cause its own problems.

The back-end process needs to be super-slick too. When a customer makes an order for delivery, whether in-store, online or on their mobile device, the order needs to be instantly redirected to the right system and location so fulfilment can begin. The process of picking the product, packing it and aggregating it in with other deliveries can start immediately.

Whichever way the system is configured, it also has to be able to withstand surges in demand. I already mentioned John Lewis and how it recruits extra staff for the Christmas season. There are other pinch-points too, and these can represent significant hurdles for a retailer. One of the most challenging is Black Friday. This marketing extravaganza first began in the

Supply chain revolution

USA in 1952. The first Friday after Thanksgiving, falling anywhere between 23 and 29 November, was seen as an opportunity to kick-start one's Christmas shopping. That tradition has now spread across the world and seems to have been adopted as an unofficial start to the festive season everywhere, with many stores competing to offer tempting discounts. Personally, I am totally against early seasonal discounting because it has educated customers to buy off-price pre-Christmas. When this was introduced into the UK by Asda in 2013, I was highly vocal about it, warning many retail CEOs of the dangers of this practice. Quite apart from the fact it cuts margin to the bone at a peak period, this not-so-mini boom puts tremendous pressure on the supply chain, with some retailers experiencing a 25% uplift in orders overnight. In the UK, it is estimated that up to £2 billion is spent over a 24-hour period. Yet, consumer expectations remain the same as at any other time of year, in terms of delivery and service. The pressure is on for retailers to build supply chain systems that are flexible enough to withstand peaks in demand.

Investing in state-of-the-art systems doesn't come cheap. Yet, however retailers decide to meet the logistics demands of the future, they need to factor in the costs of their choices because consumers are unlikely to pay for shipping for goods in a large number of categories. After all, the 'free delivery' genie is out of the lamp. If a customer can get something delivered free from elsewhere (and they generally can), it is now considered to be a competitive *dis*advantage to charge for shipping. However, this is also a changing trend. Some retailers in the UK are now charging for all deliveries, even click and collect, and this is working for them. Indeed, a growing number of retailers are realigning expectations regarding delivery timing. Boots in the UK, for example, relaxed next-day delivery in Black Friday week and produced a table showing which day the customer could expect delivery. I am sure more retailers will do this going forward.

Nevertheless, growing customer expectations mean that saving money throughout the supply chain is more crucial than ever. Once again, the digital world will come into its own. Exel, the freight-forwarding arm of DHL, is trialling 'smart glass' devices to test out vision picking in warehouses. Similar to the Google Glass concept, the internet-connected eyewear is used by workers to tell them the fastest route to find products. The devices can also read barcodes to confirm the selection is correct, and early tests show them to be able to reduce the time taken to do these things by up to 25%. However, the smart glasses come into their own for packing goods. When it comes to delivery, much of the costs are tied up in the size and weight of the package. If more prudent packing can reduce volume and minimise waste, it stands to reason that costs will reduce. The smart glasses show the packer the best possible packing configuration for goods, to minimise costs and, of course, ensure the customer receives them safely.

As the logistics of supply become ever more demanding, I believe there will be the potential for supply chain arrangements to be merged between retailers. Complementary store groups may begin working together so orders can be merged between them, to make up multi-item orders. This, in turn, presents challenges, since rival chains will have to learn to trust one another in order to be able to openly share data. However, the incentive is there. Groups of companies that can find a way to work together and collaborate meaningfully will succeed against individual enterprises that try to go it alone. A good example of this is John Lewis and Waitrose. Another is Savers, Superdrug and the Perfume Shop.

By far the largest future impact on supply chains will be the so-called internet of things (IoT). The most commonly cited example is the 'smart fridge', which can text you to tell you to bring home more milk because its internal cameras can 'see' there is no milk left. Or, better still, it could order it itself, so you can have a cuppa when you get home.

There is, however, much more to it than clever white goods. While the IoT is not new (the first internet-connected toaster was unveiled in 1989), the thinking goes that it is on the cusp of transforming the business world. The number of things being connected by the internet is growing exponentially. More than half of new business processes and systems incorporate some element of the IoT, and by 2025 the IoT will have a total potential economic impact of anywhere between $3.9 trillion and $11.1 trillion a year globally.[14]

And guess which sector is hotly tipped to be at the centre of it all. Yes, it's supply chain ecosystems. Sensors, controllers and other IoT-connected devices will find a place on everything from individual products to crates to shipping containers. They will be found in factories and warehouses and will be used to keep track of fleets of ships, trucks and automated delivery pods. Retailers will have the benefit of real-time visibility and control across their supply chains. It will be possible for orders to be entirely automated and fulfilled at any time of day or night, at double-quick time. Retailers will be

---

14   McKinsey. Internet of Things report, July 2017

able to deliver customers products before they even know they need them!

Let me give you an example. A good friend of mine lives in a remote area and uses liquid petroleum gas for heating and cooking. The gas is stored in a tank in a hole in his garden. The levels inside the tank are monitored remotely by his fuel supplier. My friend doesn't have to keep an eye on his usage. He knows that the supplier will automatically schedule a delivery when the levels are low. This works perfectly for everyone. He maintains his supply, while the fuel company can schedule multiple drops in the same area at the same time.

There are many more applications besides. In the physical store environment, smart shelves could be used to detect when inventory is low and trigger an ordering and replenishment process. Smart technology could be used in food packaging, monitoring the freshness or age of perishable goods, reducing wastage and signalling when discounts should be offered on aging stock to improve turn. Smart robots may become a common sight, working autonomously to keep shelves full of product or to assemble goods where required.

In the supply chain itself, much use will be made of RFID data. With an RFID chip in every pallet and data transferred online, the position of the shipment can be shared in real time using GPS coordinates. In turn, this data can be combined with other data, such as weather conditions and traffic reports. Imagine how cost effective it would be if delivery drivers were alerted to traffic jams or potential delays before they were already stuck in them?

By allowing devices to talk to each other, supply chain experts can:

- reduce losses, since they will know about issues early enough to find a solution;
- save fuel costs, because fleet routes can be optimised;
- manage warehouse stock and inventory, reducing out-of-stock issues;
- gain insight into customer behaviour and product usage.

Many of the futuristic examples of the IoT might feel like science fiction when you read them here, but the IoT is becoming a reality faster than you'd imagine. Retailers that take the lead in this area will benefit from the competitive advantage that is to be had from supply chain logistics. Get it right and it will be a critical pillar of any retailer's strategies, increasing revenue and reducing costs.

I strongly believe that supply chain innovation will continue to be a core focus for any retailer that wants to ensure their relevance and make sure they can respond to the insatiable demands of the modern customer.

CHAPTER CHECKOUT

✓ In a retail world where customer experience is key and the superbeings expect their items to be available *now*, it is essential for retailers to make a continuous investment in their supply chains.

✓ Today, customers have huge choice about where they can obtain their chosen items. Any retailer that doesn't immediately meet the customer's needs will lose out.

Chapter six

INVENTORY MANAGEMENT

PROFESSIONAL VIEW
How to Be a Relevant Retailer

- The secret of our brand is to lead, not to follow, but never to lead too far.
- The profit is in the buying, not in the selling.
- The profit is also the stock left on the shelf.
- Learn by small mistakes, not big ones.
- Only talk about your business, and stay focused by being true to your brand.

Ray Kelvin CBE
CEO, Ted Baker, International

Whenever I am lecturing in retail, or simply chatting to young retailers, I like to describe the three distinctive elements in our business as follows: the soul, the heart and the lifeblood.

The soul is the ambiance of any store. You can see it and easily describe it; however, there are intangible qualities too. These are what make the brand an exciting place with a distinctive point of view. Linked with this, the 'eyes' to the soul are the store windows or the retailer's website.

The heart is the buying and planning division, which pumps merchandise throughout the system and into the stores.

Without a doubt, the most important part of this entire life-support system is the lifeblood, or inventory. If a retailer does not have the right merchandise at the right price, in the right place, at the right time and in the right quantities, it will very quickly become irrelevant. In addition, if the inventory is not in line with the retailer's point of view and not purchased in line with the planned sales, the business will become bloated.

The heart can keep on pumping away as much as it likes but ultimately it will be wasting its energy if it is pumping the wrong merchandise at the wrong time or in the wrong quantities. If sell-through targets are not met, the retailer will potentially end up with an excess of merchandise at the end of the season, which is something that no retailer wants to deal with.

As I often say, no one ever went into Chapter 11 being under-stocked. They are always over-stocked, mostly with the wrong product.

In any retail operation, there are two teams that are at the centre of inventory management: the buying and merchandise planning teams. These are the people who are directly responsible for planning and executing the correct quantity of exciting products that get customers returning time and time again, fully prepared to pay full price.

Before we go into how the buying and planning functions can work together towards keeping a retailer relevant, it is worth examining just what each department does.

The buying and planning roles are, of course, very different. The buyer decides *what* to buy, while the planner decides *how much* to buy and when to deliver it. Traditionally, these roles have been referred to as the 'art' and 'science' of retailing. The thinking behind this is that the buying role is the artistic side. It is a more instinctive and creative role, based on experience and personal assessment of forthcoming trends from the 'fashion office'. Meanwhile, merchandise planning is the science, since it relies on data analytics, sales patterns and facts.

Buyers add the magic in range building. They understand that trends change, sometimes without a major indication. One day something that was red hot suddenly turns cold or vice versa. It's not always easy to predict, but buyers need to stay ahead of those trends in order to be successful.

Their skill is in knowing what is happening in the markets before they plan their orders.

Being a buyer often requires making brave decisions. You cannot back every item in the range, so you have to choose and calculate the winners. Show me a buyer who always sticks to the safe, predictable options and I'll show you one who is not succeeding.

Whenever I interview a fashion buyer, I always ask a similar question. For the sake of argument, let's imagine I am recruiting a dress buyer.

I'll ask, 'Would you rather buy six styles of dresses, twelve of each, or twelve styles of dresses, six of each?' They might respond, 'I would like to have twelve options, with six of each one.'

If this were the case, I would not be interested in employing them; they cannot edit and the key to success is to be able to edit and pick the winners.

Or, to put it another way, if you were to gamble on a horse race, it is unlikely you'd put £4 on every horse in the race. You'd bet on the potential winner, or certainly the horses you'd expect to be placed at numbers one, two and three.

The skill of a buyer is to bet on a winner and maximise the returns.

Planners, on the other hand, are highly analytical and rely on data. For this team, it is all about knowing the budget and then guiding the buyer to get the best return for money spent, while sticking within that budget. The guiding element is driven by knowing which products have sold well the previous year and in what relative proportions. Thus, for example, in fashion, the planner will know that black jumpers sold four times as many as grey ones. It therefore makes perfect sense for a planner to indicate to a buyer that if they are buying jumpers they should focus on getting in more black than grey.

Planners use fact-based assessments to rein in potential over-enthusiasm about a new trend with a realistic prediction of actual demand. Their role is to ensure buying is kept to specified, agreed hierarchies. They challenge buyers by implementing structure where chaos might otherwise exist.

RELEVANT RETAIL TIP

I have often been asked by management, specifically in fashion, about increasing intake margin, which is very important. However, I like to spend time and attention on exit margins (gross profit).

Over the years, I have attended buying reviews for forthcoming seasons where the buyers and planners present their ranges. My first question is always: What was your full-price sell-through last year and what are you planning for next season?

I am never surprised when the answer shows a large delta.

Example: last-year sell-through 42%; plan this year 65%.

Next question: 'What are you doing differently to achieve that huge improvement?'

Sadly, this is what they often don't get. As we all know, doing the same thing and expecting different results just does not work.

PROFESSIONAL VIEW
How to Be a Relevant Retailer

- Proper management of inventory has brought success to many retailers; those who lacked an understanding of its imperative have often failed.
- Retailers running off-price sales day after day are acting like a dope addict, looking for a quick fix. Once a retailer has gone down that path, it is difficult to get back to normalcy.
- Retailing is like show business. Something of excitement and interest must take place in the store to create a buying experience for the customer.
- Customer service has become a lost art. The customer is the most important part of our business. Don't ever forget it.

Ira Neimark
former Chairman and CEO Bergdorf Goodman, USA

Inventory management

I learned a valuable lesson from Ira Neimark, the former chairman and CEO of New York's famed luxury goods speciality store Bergdorf Goodman. During Ira's tenure, from 1975 to 1992, sales rose from $18 million to $250 million. With characteristic humour, he used to say he transformed the store from being somewhat 'old, dull, expensive and intimidating' to being 'young, exciting, expensive and intimidating'!

Ira kindly agreed to work with me as an adviser when I was group MD at House of Fraser in the early 1990s and, naturally, I asked him for his view on the secret to retail success.

'Andrew, you have to have tight inventory management,' he declared, without a moment's hesitation. 'If something is not selling, it is like a dead fish in a barrel. It stinks after a while.'

Ira was, of course, entirely right – and never more so than today. The days when retailers could get away with items being out of stock in the size or colour desired by the customer are over. If a customer doesn't find the product they want in a store, they can easily go elsewhere. Or, even worse, they can buy it from a retailer's rival while they are standing looking at an empty shelf. All it takes is a tap of a smartphone. There is no need for them to wait until the item comes back into stock or opt for second best. They don't have to. The time-poor customer simply doesn't have the patience to hang around or search endlessly for what they want.

CROWD PLEASER *Next, International*

Fashions come and go, but Next is a consistently well-run retailer, with class-leading margins of over 20%. This is down to an acute focus on reducing costs and managing stock levels efficiently to eliminate waste. Next's bespoke IT system ensures there is a good balance between having enough stock that customers can always get what they need, but not so much that it becomes an overstock. Warehousing and distribution are under constant review to reduce risks such as damage to goods, fabric waste, breakdowns and capacity shortages.

Inventory management is the driving force behind generating revenue and profit because sitting on un-saleable inventory ties up cash. If inventory is not carefully controlled, a retailer will spiral out of control and into irrelevance very quickly. Any retailer who wishes to remain relevant has to make inventory management a number one priority to improve sell-throughs and work towards getting *greater* return from *less* inventory.

The primary aim in this case is to avoid dead stock. These are items that cannot be sold. This might be because they are out of season or out of style, or have been acquired thanks to poor purchasing. Whatever the reason, retailers must end the season with clean inventories.

In my experience there are three key causes of overstocks:
- lack of robust 'open-to-buy' (OTB) management and control;
- lack of realistic clearance activity and markdown actions;
- lack of supply chain visibility.

Dead stock, like Ira's 'fish in a barrel', needs to be sold at a price. It clogs up warehousing, adds to storage costs and is a drain on profit. The only way to get rid of it is to sell it at a commercially marked-down price, either in the store or at an outlet. As I always say, 'there is a price for everything and the first markdown is the best one.'

No retailer can completely do away with markdowns. That is impossible. There will always be a certain amount of merchandise that can't be sold at full price. The important thing is: what percentage of goods is being sold at full price? If a retailer is only selling 40% of its goods at full price, it won't be able to make the margins to maximise the gross profit. I have always set a target of between 60% and 75% sell-through as a benchmark for businesses that I have led. Value brands should always have a higher sell-through.

The key to making sure the vast majority of stock is sold at full price is efficient management of inventory. Often senior managers miss the importance of this and, over a number of years, realise they have missed the entire boat.

The elements that enhance full-price selling are:
- editing the number of options and colours – we as merchants need to make tough choices on what we are offering our customers;
- having minimum credible offerings of assortments in-store or online to accommodate our customers' needs;
- selecting the right merchandise assortments for the season – a buyer's job is to select the winners.

RELEVANT RETAILER *H&M, International*

Five reasons why H&M's buying and planning give the chain an advantage:

Tailored assortments

The assortment mix is not just tailored to the region the range is intended for but also to the type of store. High-fashion items, such as limited editions produced in conjunction with leading designers, are only available in certain stores and in key markets. Editing is essential if you want to maximise sell-throughs. Retailers can't afford to have 'fringe' product ranges.

Fast replenishment of bestselling lines

H&M has among the highest levels of on-the-shelf availability on the high street. It has 20 sourcing offices around the world that work with around 900 suppliers. If a product sells well, H&M can act on that success and optimise it.

Price consistency

Clothes range in price from £1 to around £300, and this price point varies by less than 5% a year. Customers know to expect a well-edited range and have a clear idea of how much it will cost them.

Clear discount strategy

Around a quarter of H&M stock is discounted, with up to 10% of the range reduced by 50% or more. H&M customers are used to visiting the store to actively seek out promotions all year round.

Careful curating of brand identity

H&M uses 'storytelling' techniques to portray its brand and create looks. Online, for example, it has switched from flat, clickable product images with a price point and a 'shop now' link. Instead, it groups products using a magazine format, with stylised imagery and mood-setting text.

H&M, Melbourne – Flagship store curating a strong brand identity

RETAIL GRAVEYARD *Austin Reed, UK*

Five reasons why poor buying and merchandising led to the downfall of Austin Reed:

Forgotten heritage

Austin Reed's inventory made nothing of the chain's more than 100 years of heritage. Instead, it stuck to 'safe', yet nondescript, bland shirting and standard corporate suits.

Ignored modern tastes

At the other end of the scale, there was no nod whatsoever to contemporary tastes. Uninspiring garments failed to shine against modern retailers such as Ted Baker.

Failed to inspire young customers

Younger men should have been a crucial market to Austin Reed, since they spend more money on suits and update their style regularly. However, the chain seemed content to target its ageing customer base.

Poor store layouts

Shops were merchandised by product rather than look, which left the impression that style was not an important consideration. The jackets were all in one place, the ties in another. Modern shoppers prefer to buy 'looks'.

Eclipsed by trend for bespoke

Austin Reed failed to recognise, or emulate, the trend for quality suits and bespoke services, promoted by services such as ASuitThatFits.com and Savile Row tailors, which offer affordable, high-quality, bespoke suits.

While the buyer and planner are separate and need to report into different department heads, the two disciplines must work together in harmony to keep the business running to optimum effect. If you have the chief merchant in charge of planners then you have the fox in charge of the hen house. In my experience, the planning function ideally needs to report to the CFO. OTB control is critically important, and hence involvement from the finance department is essential. Too many large organisations base their OTB for the next season on *achieved sales*, including markdowns, rather than full-price sell-throughs, which is clearly a recipe for disaster.

A planner might need to use their research to temper a buyer's excitement about a novel, fun or exciting product that seems innovative but that few customers might actually buy. By the same token, buyers can use their creativity to dissuade planners from too often erring towards the 'safe' option. Without this balance, planners can easily fall into the trap of always preferring perhaps basic, or core, products that are known to sell well. Such choices are logical and easy to formulate; however, they don't give the retailer the wow factor that they require. And they certainly won't guarantee relevancy.

When the buyer–planner partnership is optimised, a retailer will not only benefit from better sell-throughs but also increase their margins. If, on the other hand, planners run the show, the inventory may well appear perfect on paper, but sadly the sales will probably not match because there is too little creativity. The balance has to be just right to succeed.

The best way to achieve synergy between buyers and planners is by:

- Communication: planners and buyers should be in constant contact and working closely together as a team.
- Integration: data should flow seamlessly between departments and be accessible to all levels.
- Discipline: checks and balances are needed at all stages of the process to keep things under control as well as to keep inventory margins and gross sales on track.
- Alignment: it is vital to ensure that people, processes and systems are optimised to deliver the vision and the strategy in terms of right product, right price, right place, at the right time to the customer on the shop floor.

In my experience, this alignment is often hampered by a lack of understanding of how the different functions need to work together. Other factors include not sharing information and a failure to understand how the decisions made in one area can significantly impact the costs throughout the supply chain and ultimately the sales to the customer.

From a retail perspective, these challenges are compounded when you are creating and managing your own brand ranges.

There is no one-size-fits-all process model, and most businesses will have a number of models depending on the type of product sold, where the suppliers are based and the supply chain logistics.

Cross-functional teams from all of the relevant functions should be involved in building the detailed processes so that everyone understands who is doing what and when. This enables the various functions to work quickly and effectively in teams to deliver customer-focused ranges.

The benefits are very substantial, not only in terms of customer satisfaction, sales and profit but also in the many other areas, such as:

- reduced costs in the supply chain;
- ability to shorten lead times;
- ability to manage stock and improve stockturns;
- improved team working;
- clear accountabilities and hard performance measures;
- consistency of approach through training.

This is a great learning process for many of the people involved. When I've instigated new initiatives in this respect, I've often got comments like, 'I have been working as a buyer for nine years and this is the first time I have really understood how our supply chain works!' People often don't realise how their decisions can impact other people or functions.

Getting inventory management right involves everybody in the business, including finance, HR, training, stores, supply chain and logistics. This sets a great base for developing a programme for ongoing improvements in speed to market and cost reduction, as well as the ability to adapt to changes in the marketplace.

As any retailer will attest, a harmonious relationship between buying and planning is not always easy to achieve. Indeed, a silo mentality often ensues, where one or the other side will freeze the other out and do their best to get on with their own task unhindered or unencumbered by the views of the other.

While the relationship takes some skill to manage, it is essential that both departments exist. In 2010, when I was appointed the CEO of the ailing German department store chain Karstadt, I discovered there was no separate merchandise planning division at all. Karstadt, which had 83 stores, appeared to be following a very traditional route of stocking what its competition had, or buying more of what it bought the previous year. There was no focus on the customer and no understanding of who the buyers were buying for. The net result was zero differentiation from any other store on the high street. Karstadt didn't have a point of view and customers knew it. No wonder the chain was in trouble.

My strategy to revamp Karstadt boiled down to four key components:

- modernising the image;
- differentiating the assortment and tightly managing inventories;
- sharpening the processes;
- simplifying the ways of working.

The key to achieving this was to take apart the traditional buying function and build a professional merchandise planning division that would act as a partner to the buyers on an equal footing.

Once I'd restructured the buying and merchandising divisions, I had to come up with a plan for how to help the groups work together in closer, more efficient ways. The goal was to get better thinking, better decisions and better end results. Above all, I wanted an inclusive, cooperative and collaborative environment.

I set a challenge for each department. Planners were asked to begin with a post-season review, gathering intelligence and feedback from both buying and store teams to learn valuable lessons from what had gone before. These lessons learned were an important part of next season's range reviews. Buyers were encouraged to take in information from a wider sphere of influence, from customer research to partners overseas to planning data. Both departments were also guided to liaise more closely with the marketing department so as to make marketing aware of the new products that were on the way and also to facilitate themed promotions and events around the new ranges. Collaboration was key.

To explain what I was trying to achieve, I introduced the Karstadt team to one of my favourite retail analogies: the kettle inventory management principle. It is a very simple, yet effective, illustration of how the merchandising process works. I will share it with you here too:

Imagine a store as a kettle. You are about to use that kettle to boil water to make a satisfying brew for your customers. The water, or stock, needs to be poured into the kettle to precisely the right level. If you put in too much water, it will cost far more to heat it and you'll be left with a lot of hot water. The resources used in your promotional fire will be wasted. Too little water, though, and you may not have enough to fill the customers' cups and some people will be left disappointed.

Inventory management

It is vital that planning never stops the flow, or pipeline, of merchandise, so there is always the optimum level of water/stock in the business. The challenge is to control the tap so that the flow of goods is in balance with the needs of the customer.

Sadly, as everyone knows, no matter how careful you are, there will always be an accumulation of small particles, or limescale, at the bottom of a kettle. It is important to keep rinsing them out, in order to keep the brew fresh. The same goes for stock. No matter how efficient and aligned the buying and merchandising process, there will always be an accumulation of unsold stock, which sinks to the bottom and ages. It is crucial to regularly wash it out of the inventory by using markdowns. After all, it is inconvenient having to spring clean a thoroughly clogged up kettle! Keep on top of it to ensure everything keeps flowing smoothly.

Finally, at the risk of pushing the kettle analogy too far, I should add that it is far better to fill our kettle with *hot* water (the wanted items). Hot water boils more quickly and requires less fuel (promotional money) to do so. Cold water, or slow sellers, requires more time and energy and is ultimately less cost effective.

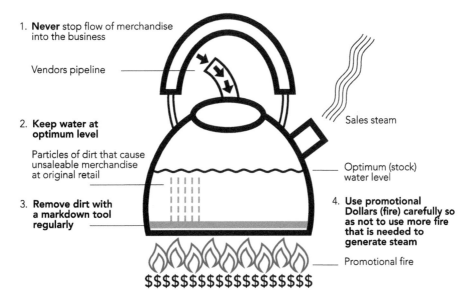

1. **Never** stop flow of merchandise into the business

Vendors pipeline

2. **Keep water at optimum level**

Particles of dirt that cause unsaleable merchandise at original retail

3. **Remove dirt with a markdown tool regularly**

Sales steam

Optimum (stock) water level

4. **Use promotional Dollars (fire) carefully so as not to use more fire that is needed to generate steam**

Promotional fire

Figure 2. The kettle principle of inventory management

PROFESSIONAL VIEW
How to Be a Relevant Retailer

- A store must be exciting in the way it is merchandised.
- A store *must* have a real point of difference.
- The merchant should ensure they can surprise and delight their customers every time the customers walk into the store.
- The shopping experience must be memorable.

William Lauder
Executive Chairman, The Estée Lauder Companies, International

---

The next logical step in inventory control is to use digital technology to buy and plan on the basis of what is happening right now, rather than in terms of what customers bought last year.

Modern technology has contributed greatly to the efficiencies of merchandising, and the information to which retailers have access improves all the time. Understanding what stock you need and where it has to be is a scenario that can change daily, even hourly, depending on a range of variables such as weather, holidays, promotions and competitor actions. It is now possible to get instant feedback on the rate of sale of specific products for any given day or week. Planners will know immediately if a selection is selling and will be fully equipped to make an informed decision as to whether to mark a range of products down rather than risk being left with a large holding at the end of the season. Feedback on sales can be used as a scientific basis for adjusting decisions along the way, before they turn into a real problem later on.

Thus, to take the earlier example, if the grey and pink sweaters unexpectedly prove to sell faster than the black, a retailer will be alert to the trend very early on. It can then put black sweaters on promotion and reorder more grey, to make sure the season ends cleanly in this department and potential losses are minimised.

Spanish retailer Zara is a great example of a chain that uses this strategy brilliantly. It systematically examines early sales data to predict potential demand for specific clothing lines. Sales trends are then scrutinised at regular intervals throughout the sales cycle and any fast-moving items are swiftly re-ordered. Perhaps not surprisingly, Zara's gross margin return on inventory investments is higher than the industry average.

Inventory management

A number of other retailers are now also using this sort of 'predictive analytics' to produce smart, lean assortments that consistently offer shoppers what they are looking for, in the colours and styles that work for them. Strangely, though, considering the amount of available data, this is still far from the norm.

It's not uncommon for retailers, particularly fashion chains, to blame 'unseasonal' weather for poor sales in a season. This can in part be avoided by using transitional colours, weights and styles during the months of August–September and February–March (at the beginning of each season). As forecasting technology improves (and it is getting better all the time), shops should increasingly be using it to refine their inventories.

While forecasting techniques are not particularly new, they are still significantly under-used when retailers are calculating demand projections. Retailers often use them for buy-one-get-one-free promotions, or marketing pushes, yet they are not used enough in planning and supply chain predictions. In the digital age, a dynamic ability to forecast demand is increasingly critical. Sales surges happen at lightning speed. Retailers need to be ready to meet demand.

Predictive analytics doesn't just operate in real time either. As the name suggests, it is also concerned with the future. Indeed, used correctly, it can be the retail equivalent of a crystal ball. There are a plethora of potential information sources available at our fingertips: social trends, psychology, economics and many other tools can offer clues about the quantity, type and mix of inventory we hold. Every time customers look at a website, call a contact centre, redeem an offer or use a loyalty card, they leave behind a wealth of valuable information about themselves, their shopping preferences and their potential buying patterns.

Predictive analytics can be used to plan for both the long and the short term. For example, we know that the British shopper is hugely sensitive to changes in the weather. A change in temperature of just a degree or two, either way, can increase sales of some lines by as much as 400% over a short period. One survey found that weather forecast information could boost sales by £4.5 billion a year in the UK grocery and clothing sector.[15] For example, a supermarket could plan a buy-one-get-one-free promotion of a branded ice cream for a period when hot weather is predicted. Or a fashion

---

15   Datamonitor/Met Office. Retail Monitor

store could stock up on wet-weather gear if a damp autumn is on the cards.

Predictive analytics is often a particular bonus for internet retailers when it comes to inventory management and is another area where they can race ahead against their high street counterparts.

Another area of predictive analytics that has proven hugely successful is in product recommendations. Again, this has been particularly successful for online retailers. Amazon was a pioneer in recommending choices based on predictive models. Most consumers will be very familiar with online prompts such as 'you bought X, so you may also like Y'. People often express amazement at the accuracy of the ideas, which chime perfectly with their tastes. However, they stem merely from an (albeit complex) algorithm that uses search history.

Bricks-and-mortar retailers need not despair. There are significant opportunities for them in predictive analytics too. Experts have turned their attention to the customer journey in-store and used technology to map how people shop. Once retailers are in possession of this information, the next logical step is to alter layouts to 'lead' customers to where you need them, thus aiding the buying process.

To better understand how people shop, shopping trollies and baskets can be tagged with radio-frequency identification tags to assess shopper movement. This information can be put together with point-of-sale data and 'market basket analysis' to piece together the puzzle of why people buy what they do. US department store group Macy's used this information in its research and created a virtual store model where it experimented with different layouts and staffing based on expected store traffic and customer journeys.

Although it is one of the oldest adages in the book, maximising revenue per customer is still fundamentally important today, and insights like these go a long way towards achieving this all-important goal.

CROWD PLEASER *Sainsbury's, UK*

Sainsbury's used a predictive computer model to track customer movement around one test store in West London. The supermarket used the information it gained to test alternative layouts. Different departments, such as frozen foods and the deli counter, were moved to trial the effect of layout changes on sales. Sainsbury's found that separating 'high-traffic' areas, such as the meat and deli sections, encouraged impulse buying elsewhere, as customer moved between these 'hot spots'. The study also showed that when customers felt the store was too busy, less wine was sold. Fewer customers were prepared to make their way over to the wine section, which was located in the far corner.

When it comes to managing inventory, it should be noted that technology is not the only tool we have at our disposal. We can have access to all the best predictive analytics in the world, but I would argue that nothing should ever replace the evidence that is often there before your very own eyes.

Shortly after I took over at House of Fraser, I did a tour of the retailer's stores around the UK. I will never forget my experience in the Sheffield store. When I'd glanced over the sales figures prior to my visit, I hadn't been able to help noticing that this store's suit business was unusually poor, and so one of my first ports of call was the menswear department.

The sales team all seemed pleasant enough and the department was tidy and well stocked. In fact, all seemed fine at first glance, except there was not a single customer in sight.

I cornered one of the assistants, who was busily re-arranging a display.

After introducing myself, I said, 'I have a magic wand here to increase sales. If I passed it over to you, what would you use it for?'

He smiled. 'I'd get the right size suit assortment,' he said, without hesitation.

'Please explain,' I prompted.

'Well, there is a steel foundry just up the road,' he began. 'Many of the men in this area work there. It's tough, physical work, which means the guys who work there have big chests. There is no way they can fit into any of the suits we stock, since they are all too narrow. The buyers up in London don't have a clue.'

It was a big lesson, and the moment I got back to central office I called the buyers together and we began to work on a plan to localise our ranges. We also began to communicate a lot better as a company. It was all a vital part of giving our customers what they wanted and keeping our inventory flowing.

Reducing wasted inventory will not only keep a retailer relevant but also save millions. It will also give a huge intangible boost to a brand, since, in this more socially conscious world, wastage is frowned upon.

CHAPTER CHECKOUT

✓ Take timely markdowns on slow sellers.

✓ Too many executives focus on markdowns – always focus on sell-throughs.

✓ Make sure your full-price sell-throughs are maximised. Always set buyers and planners key performance indicators in this area.

✓ Create a detailed business process model with clear accountabilities and responsibilities.

✓ Buying and planning need to work as a team.

✓ Set up a buying and merchandising academy to ensure there is engagement in the discipline you require.

✓ Don't forget that people on the ground in-store have amazing insights.

Chapter seven

TALENT

I still remember my excitement as I began my career in retail. I was a management trainee within the Debenhams organisation and embarked on a four-year training programme that covered everything from buying to merchandising and marketing to finance.

I didn't think twice about the lowlier aspects of being a trainee, even though I did the whole range of these, including being a bag carrier, doing housekeeping chores and carrying out much grunt work. I was already in love with the retail industry. My passion was rewarded by my employers and I progressed through the ranks, from running stores to running regions to eventually becoming Head of Fashion Buying and then Head of Marketing. I eventually became a COO and then a CEO in various geographies and was privileged to run some of the world's most famous retail brands.

The challenge for the industry today is to enthuse talent like my younger self in a sector that has less to offer than many others. It is a challenge we need to meet. I have highlighted many new innovations in this book as well as advances in technology and in the way we do business. However powerful all of these new innovations are, though, they are nothing without good, talented people behind them. Retail is still very much a people business. We have to recruit the best people, develop them and most importantly listen to them.

I always describe myself as a student of retail. By this I mean I am constantly on the alert for new ideas, different solutions and advances in technology. My quest to fully understand the needs of customers is never ending.

The best source of information is, without a doubt, people. While some people readily befriend cats and dogs, I like to befriend store managers, ecommerce experts, social-media-minded folk and customers in stores. In fact, anyone who has an opinion about shops and shopping is immediately on my radar. I interact with such individuals regularly and listen very, very hard to what they tell me about their business and experiences. What works? What doesn't? What do customers love? What couldn't they care less about?

It was in this way that I came into contact with an extraordinarily talented young person who, in a very vivid way, illustrated to me the one element that is the most important characteristic of shop staff. That characteristic is passion.

I met this individual while I was still based in New York, working as president of Saks Fifth Avenue. At the end of another long day, my wife Karen met me in my office beside the store and we travelled together to a very chic restaurant for dinner. We'd not visited this particular restaurant before but had decided to give it a try on the recommendation of friends. The tip turned out to be excellent and we spent a very memorable evening.

It wasn't just the food that created the impression, although the dishes were first rate. No, on this particular occasion, it was the service that was outstanding. This was principally down to our waitress. Tracy was everything a great waitress should be: attentive, efficient and knowledgeable, yet something more besides. She had a charming and engaging character and was passionate about both the restaurant and the work she did there. Looking around at the other tables that Tracy was also serving, I could see she had made an impression on the other diners too.

Tracy and I got chatting at the end of the evening as I settled our bill. She told me that she was an actress and moonlighted as a waitress in between jobs as so many in her profession often do. She admitted she was at a bit of a crossroads in her life and wasn't sure whether she should stick with the acting at all.

'What is it you'd like to do?' I asked. I was genuinely interested in the answer.

She paused for a moment, as though unsure whether she should say. I nodded in encouragement.

'My real passion is looking after and serving customers, believe it or not,' she said. 'I really get a kick out of helping people and making sure they get what they want.'

I couldn't help smiling as I handed her my business card and told her I was president at Saks.

'I think we might be able to help each other,' I said. 'Give me a call.'

A short while later, Tracy called me and I invited her to meet our recruitment team at Saks for a more formal discussion. Shortly after that, we gave her a job as a personal shopper in the Fifth Avenue Club.

Just as I expected, Tracy did not let me down. Despite having no previous retail experience, her passion and character shone through. In her first year at the store, she made more than a million dollars in sales. Passion truly is the human soul on fire.

I have long been a fervent believer that people are the most important asset in our business, and this experience added to that conviction. The right team can make or break companies.

PROFESSIONAL VIEW
How to Be a Relevant Retailer

- Believe in the magic of people – never be afraid to hire smarter, brighter people around you.
- Keep close – keeping close to your customers, suppliers and staff is vital. Never let the scale of a business get in the way of you keeping close to your stakeholders.
- Retail *really is* detail, as the famous aphorism goes. There's no substitute for keeping on top of the detail. If you don't, your competitors will.
- Value is vital – retailers might sell expensive stuff, but everything they sell must come with a deep sense of value for money.

Ewan Venters
CEO, Fortnum & Mason, UK

People are a key deciding factor in relevancy – now more than ever. Modern consumers have ever-higher expectations of their shopping experience. They demand more personalised attention and this manifests itself in a number of ways, not least an expectation that retail employees 'walk the talk'. In other words, staff are not just there to stock the store and process transactions. They fulfil a role as ambassadors and need to be infinitely knowledgeable about everything from the products they sell to current trends in the market and, of course, the company they represent. Indeed, it could be said that the customer expects retailers to be less like sales staff and more like consultants.

PROFESSIONAL VIEW
How to Be a Relevant Retailer

- Be prepared to move good people aside and to replace them with excellent people. They alone will drive your business forward.
- Trust your gut and be very well informed. Never stop asking and your gut will keep you on track.

Talent

- Make your business one year younger every year otherwise it and your customers will grow old with you.
- The truth of a retail business is in the stores, and the stores are now also in cyberspace.

Simon Susman
Chairman, Woolworths Holdings, South Africa

Don't forget either that customers are exceptionally well informed too nowadays, thanks to the digital world. The bar has moved significantly higher and any assistant who does not match up to expectations, or who disappoints the customer with their lack of knowledge, will inevitably spoil the experience.

Plus, as if this were not enough of a challenge, the growth of cross-channel, or omnichannel, retailing places another element in the mix to test the strength of the team. The experience at the physical store of Brand X needs to be the same as the experience at the online version of Brand X every time. There is only one way this can be achieved, though: through the team. They need to live the brand and exude it at every turn.

Most of all, though, there is one element of team behaviour that should stand head and shoulders above the rest. It is more important than knowledge and expertise, or a smooth brand transition between platforms, although each are crucial. It is the quality I saw in Tracy: passion. Customers today want the people they deal with to be passionate about the products they sell. With so much choice on offer and so many outlets offering similar products, the venue that seems to understand and value the customer the most will always be a winner.

I've got tangible proof that this is the case, too. At Saks Fifth Avenue, we conducted research and found customers would spend 17% more if they had a trusted relationship with a sales associate. Without a doubt, staff are a retailer's most important asset. This is why I spend so much of my time and energy recruiting and training my retail teams (and, believe me, if I could have cloned Tracy, I would!).

CROWD PLEASER *Mitchells Stores, USA*

Founded in 1958 in Westport, Connecticut, Mitchells Stores'
success is based on 'hugs'. Not the touchy-feely kind, but in
the way the team gets close to customers with passion and
commitment towards extraordinary customer service. In its
simplest form, a hug is anything that exceeds a customer's
expectations, such as a smile or handshake. A big hug is a letter
of thanks. Team members are encouraged to develop long-term
relations with customers. The value works because everyone in
the organisation, from top to bottom, fully buys into it.

Sadly, many retailers seriously underestimate the power of their talent.
They see staff as a cost. To understand how little shop assistants are valued,
you only have to look at how the structure of the retail employer–employee
relationship has changed dramatically over the past few years. So-called jobs
for life were consigned to the history books a long time ago, but in recent
years we have just seen a further massive shift away from such staples of
the past. Zero-hours contracts, subcontracting, temporary contracts, part-
time agreements: non-standard employment is the new standard when it
comes to retailers. Store group leaders have become increasingly inventive
in creating flexibility for themselves while weakening worker protections.
Some companies in particular, such as Amazon, Sports Direct, Walmart and
numerous internet start-ups, have fully embraced subcontracting as the
perfect way to get labour on demand. The argument goes that it is great for
workers too because they benefit from fantastic job flexibility and can build
their job around their personal schedules.

There are more than 2.9 million people working in the retail sector in the
UK, making it the nation's biggest employer.[16] In the USA, retail directly and
indirectly supports 42 million jobs, providing $1.6 trillion in labour income.[17]
This represents a lot of people who may be feeling unsure or insecure about
their job prospects in this sector. The employment environment adds up to
too many people feeling demoralised and fed up about what should be the
best job in the world.

---

16   Office for National Statistics, *Labour Force Survey*, 2017
17   Bureau of Labor Statistics, *Retail Trade*, 2016

CROWD PLEASER *Asda, UK*

Asda, the UK subsidiary of supermarket giant Walmart, has a core value of respect for its employees (known as colleagues). There are formal and informal structures for rewarding employees who behave in the required way. Rewards include a range of perks such as child-friendly policies (where parents can take additional leave over the summer to take care of school-aged children), career-break options and study leave (where colleagues can develop interests elsewhere). Staff are given extensive coaching and feedback, and are offered company share ownership plans and a range of other financial benefits. Colleague Circles is a forum for staff involvement in customer service innovation. Its 'Caring for our Customers' scheme rewards the best examples of good service and every month each store selects a Gold Service Hero. Each of these actions is designed to support the respect of a colleague's value.

Let's begin with recruitment.

As a starting point, a retailer needs to think carefully about the sort of candidate it needs. Passion and commitment are, I hope, a given. But what other talents are required?

While it is tempting to focus on a particular skill set – say, a technology retailer might look for people who are tech-wizards, or a Millennial-orientated fashion store might focus on someone with a quirky style – I'd issue a note of caution here. There needs to be a good mixture of people in any team.

I often use the analogy of a box of Nestlé Quality Street chocolates when I explain this to my senior teams (and bring along a box of them too, which always goes down well).

I'd tip the brightly coloured contents of the box out onto the table and say something like this: 'In this box of Quality Street, you'll find soft-centred ones, nutty ones, chewy ones and some with hard centres. This is just like a good team. If you want a Quality Street Gang, you need to recruit people with different skill sets. Everyone brings something new to the table and each person's skill adds to the whole. Over the years, I have always looked to recruit top and middle management teams who complement each other. The important thing is that there is collaboration and a synergistic approach.

Everyone should feed off the energy and talents of each other. It is the sum of the parts that makes us special.'

The obvious retort is: retail is not a 'sexy' business. Salaries are not particularly impressive and contracts offer little job security. How are we going to attract these passionate people with all their varying talents? In addition, the flip side to our new era of short-term contracts is that we now live in a free-agent society. Not only is it more difficult to attract the best candidates but it is also harder to keep them. If people are going to commit to an employer that barely commits to them, there needs to be something quite special on the table.

The answer is, of course, to show potential candidates just what an exciting, stimulating and intoxicating place retail can be. We need to encourage them to feel passion about dealing with the public and helping them to find the goods they want to buy.

Some pockets of retail already have a head start in this endeavour and are already perceived to be sexy. In February 2013, for example, 1701 applicants battled for just three full-time and five part-time barista jobs at a new Costa in Nottingham, UK. Many of those people had more than 15 years retail experience. It wasn't the money on offer that made the job so desirable. Even a fully qualified 'barista maestro' only commands a salary just above minimum wage. No, it is the fact that being a barista has almost become a fashion statement. There is a cachet to working in these coffee shops and it means the owners have the pick of the bunch. Imagine if that cachet could be transferred to other retail outlets?

In some cases, though, retailers will have to fight for the best people. I recall a very appropriate quote from the Sunday Business Section of the *New York Times* written by management professor John J. Sullivan, who said: 'There is a new war for talent, but most companies aren't bothering to fight. Whether it is a store manager, or a software developer, there is a huge gap between the business results that average employees deliver and what stars deliver. If you want to win the battle in the product market, you have to win the battle in the talent market.'[18]

There are many things that can be done, and the more creative and innovative the better.

Being active on social media and on blogs is essential when trying to

18   *New York Times*, 26 April 2006

attract young talent. When Karstadt launched a recruitment campaign on Facebook in 2014, we did just this and had 2000 people apply for student and trainee jobs in just three days.

There are other things that you can do to make your interview process so exciting that prospective staff can't help but come along to take a look. The aim is to get them intrigued by what your organisation has to offer and then it is up to you to persuade them that you are everything they hoped you'd be.

This was certainly the approach I adopted while recruiting new store assistants for Holt Renfrew in Toronto. Upon deciding that the theatrical touch was just what we needed for the then recently revamped flagship speciality store, I set up a series of 'auditions' for new staff. By auditions, I mean the sort of stage test that aspiring actors have to go through in order to win a part in a play or show. The event was widely advertised in the media and colleagues were also encouraged to spread the word of this unusual recruitment fair. Aspiring candidates were asked to pre-submit application forms and we chose 200 potential new 'cast' members. The would-be new staff were given a script or role-play scenario, according to the department they'd applied for, and asked to look them over ahead of their audition slot.

On the day of the auditions themselves, which were held on a Sunday morning, we dressed the flagship store entrances like a film set using lighting and bespoke signage. We even had a red carpet and movie cameras outside on the street to greet the rather surprised auditionees. On arrival, each candidate was given a t-shirt to commemorate their participation in the 'production', a bottle of water and a goodie bag. We showed them around the store and then led them to their chosen department, where existing shop assistants and managers acted out the other side in the role play.

Hardly surprisingly, the strategy was a huge success. We had an exceptional standard of would-be recruits to choose from. Indeed, many of them were outstanding.

Naturally, I was at the audition event too and I made sure I had a one-to-one session with each of the shortlisted candidates. This was thanks to another lesson I learned from Wolf Hengst, the Global President of the Four Seasons hotel group.

'Andrew, when we open a hotel, our general managers have to personally interview every single person, from the chambermaid up, twice,' he told me. 'They need to make sure they have the right people. We are like a family.'

I have always tried to have that same perspective. Anyone who comes into a business I run has to want to be part of it. Attitude, like passion, is crucial.

RELEVANT RETAILER *Zappos, USA*

Five reasons why online fashion store Zappos offers the best customer service thanks to its people:

Interviews value weirdness as much as skills

Zappos has a strong set of core company values, which include 'create fun and a little weirdness'. The recruitment process involves two interviews: one to assess fit with the job and the other to assess cultural fit with the company. Candidates are asked: 'On a scale of one to ten, how weird are you?' The number doesn't matter – it is more a question to ensure that the interviewee understands that Zappos recognises and celebrates individuality.

Money where its mouth is

Zappos offers new employees a $4000 cash bonus to leave after their four-week training period is up. The idea is that unmotivated hires go quickly while those who stay do so in the knowledge that the company cares deeply about providing good service and nurturing ability. Around 2–3% take the cash.

Those who don't fit the culture are out

Even if a person is smart, talented and qualified, they will be let go if they are bad for the company culture. Around 50% of Zappos' performance reviews are based on whether the team member is living and inspiring the company culture in others. And, as we all know, what gets measured gets done.

It's about time, not money

Most call centres use a metric called 'average handle time' to gauge their efficiency. Zappos, which is focused on great customer service, trusts their customer service reps to make their own decisions. One of its longest call times was 10 hours and 29 minutes! The company philosophy is, if they have a customer's undivided attention for even five minutes, it is the equivalent of a five-minute-long Zappos infomercial that people are paying attention to.

Decisions come from the front lines

There are no set policies. Staff on the front lines are asked to do whatever they feel is right for the individual customers. Bureaucracy is kept to a minimum.

It is easy to get tied up with wanting excellent skills and qualifications. While these are important, they are not the be-all and end-all. Indeed, if I am hiring someone who will be interacting with customers on the shop floor, I'll hire for attitude every time. They need to be smart, yes, but they also need to be street smart. If they don't have entirely the right qualifications or skills, you can always train them. As I always say: hire for attitude, train for skill and aptitude.

The right mindset is so important. It makes such a huge difference to the end result. I often use the analogy of the Olympics when I explain this to my senior teams. I adore the Olympics and look forward to it every four years with great anticipation. My favourite part is watching the post-event interviews with the gold medallists. It is here that you see what makes these people extraordinary. For a few moments you get a brief glimpse into what they have been through in the lead-up to that moment when they surged over the winning line in triumph. These athletes have undergone 12 hours a day of intense training, day in and day out, month after month, and now it has all come together. They went through all that because they had a passion and determination to win and a fervent belief that they could do so. Now that is a winning mindset!

Nordstrom, Toronto – Contemporary lounge for fitting rooms

While I don't expect all of my recruits to be gold-medal material, I want them to feel they can be the best and, better still, that my organisation is the place where they want to hone and improve their skills as they strive towards perfection.

The interview process is an extremely important part of talent selection. Over the years, I have always ensured that, once we've got an idea that a candidate has what it takes, we go on to hold a second interview in a store to gain an understanding of how the potential executive relates to the 'front line'. I do this for positions from CFOs to supply chain executives. I have also found great value in the use of psychometric assessments as part of the selection process. They really do assist both parties to see whether the fit is right.

CROWD PLEASER *Nordstrom, USA and Canada*

Nordstrom is an international retailer with more than 250 stores in the USA and Canada. The business grew out of one store in Seattle, which was founded in 1901 with the cornerstone value of 'best-in-class customer service'.

The stated responsibility of each employee is to please the customer. Indeed, for many years, the company employee handbook, which was handed to each new member of staff, had just one rule: 'Nordstrom Rules: Rule 1: Use your good judgment in all situations. There will be no additional rules.'

Once you've recruited great people, you have to make them even better and then go on supporting them to continuously improve. I often say: sales teams are like storage batteries, constantly discharging energy. It is our job to re-energise them with support, product knowledge and enthusiasm to create a spirit that builds the culture in a company. Our industry is already feeling the pain of neglecting this crucially important requirement. We lose too many of our best and brightest to other industries. If we want to make retailing a preferred career choice and recruit the best people to help us stay relevant, the industry has to step up.

High-quality training and development should be a priority for any organisation. I am a huge believer in development. Turning good people into great people requires a mixture of commitment, coaching and support plus a good dash of inspiration.

This doesn't just mean on-the-job training, or a half-hour morning session every month or so. To keep people interested (and therefore work towards relevance), a retail business needs to commit to the continuous development of its talent. At Saks Fifth Avenue, we took colleagues to the West Coast of America to immerse them in how people in Silicon Valley worked. We visited Facebook, Google and Microsoft and our people saw first hand how these other forward-thinking businesses worked. The team returned to New York with dozens of innovative ideas for novel ways to integrate technology into their everyday work and to improve even the simplest of tasks. I also arranged a bespoke programme with the Center for Creative Leadership in Colorado Springs, which dozens of our senior team attended.

When I worked with Woolworths in South Africa, we had a business relationship with Marks and Spencer and I arranged a 'swap programme', where members of my team spent time in the UK, working in management positions at M&S. I wanted them to benefit from a different and hopefully inspiring way of working. Regional managers were exposed to running UK stores and they learned new skills very quickly.

Shops should foster a creative environment where team members can share ideas and examples of best practice. If anyone has good ideas, and they always do, there should be a mechanism, or indeed more than one, where they can let others hear about them. Likewise, if any initiatives are being introduced, or considered elsewhere in the business, the senior team should share them throughout the ranks. I've always been a big fan of town-hall-style meetings, where everyone in each store gets together to hear some words from the company leadership.

It is crucial that the efforts of the team are recognised at every opportunity. Saying thank you and recognising a job well done goes a long way. Researchers have proven that when you thank someone, it makes them more relaxed, collaborative and happy. Reward and recognition strategies need to be ingrained in a company's DNA to drive discretionary effort and inspire a team to do more. It is no coincidence that, consistently over time, 70% of the *Sunday Times*' top 100 employers invest in reward and recognition programmes. People want to work for employers who appreciate their talent.

I have always believed in, and seen the returns from, meaningful events to recognise talent. I've run numerous occasions, from 'Night of the Stars' to recognition lunches, dinners or breakfasts. On these occasions, the most deserving members of the team are rewarded with awards and gift vouchers. Initiatives like this are not just inspiring for the recipients of the recognition. They perk up the rest of the team too, who all work harder because they all aspire to be part of the celebration in the future.

During my very first 'Stars Luncheon' at a retail business in Durban, South Africa, we recognised one of the most talented young menswear salesmen, a man called Ali Aziz. People would often say that Ali would 'swim the bay' for his customers, meaning there was nothing he wouldn't consider in order to give them the best possible service. Birthday cards, personal home deliveries and even home wardrobe reviews were all part of his personal added value for his customers.

Ali always exceeded his targets and became the best all-round menswear salesman in the region. His focus was: 'Keep every one of my customers happy and they will come back time and time again.'

We racked our brains as to how we could recognise Ali for his 'out of this world' service and decided on an innovative prize. We purchased a star in the galaxy in his name through the International Star Registry in Switzerland. Ali was presented with a framed ornate certificate at the Stars Luncheon and he was thrilled with the prize. He went on to become a successful senior executive within the business.

These recognition events are another great way for the retail leadership to speak directly to the team. I truly believe that listening to people who have interactions with customers is the most valuable thing we can do at any stage of our retail careers.

I have always loved visiting stores and still do. When I was group MD at House of Fraser, I spent at least every Saturday out in the stores. I would often fly to Glasgow, Birmingham or Manchester, visit a couple of stores there, return to London and visit the Oxford Street flagship store, and then finish the day in Barkers in Kensington High Street, which was near to my home. Lesley, the store manager there, was so used to my routine that she'd keep the shop open beyond its 7.30pm closing time, just so she could walk me around. What's more, she was so passionate about what she did, she didn't mind one bit. I always looked forward to her updates.

RELEVANT RETAIL TIP

Some retail organisations have evolved to be built on so many layers that those near the bottom of the chain of command (the people in the stores) barely know what the leadership looks like, let alone what makes them tick. If a company leader only interacts with their direct reports, who in turn only speak to the next layer down and so on, the cultural message gets diluted each time. Not only that, but there is a lack of clarity about what is happening on the front line.

There is little point setting the values and behaviours that will drive your growth if a large chunk of your workforce has no clue this process has gone on at all. Leaders need to get wired into the culture so everyone in the company knows and understands the parts that each other play.

It has always been my philosophy to ensure that everyone is on the same page and is crystal clear on the objectives to be achieved.

Interfacing with the customer is the moment of truth for any retailer. As a retail leader, you learn so much from the people on the front line and, when asked the right questions, they will tell you everything. Show me a retail executive who does not go out into their stores and I will show you someone who will not be successful.

It is crucial that the in-store team feels empowered to speak up and share their own ideas. If something works, tell everyone. Similarly, if something doesn't work, tell everyone too. No one should be afraid to speak up about failures. I have had my fair share of failures over the years and I have always learned from them. It is important, though, to fail quickly and only do so once. I often say, 'It's fine to make a mistake and learn from it; however, don't make the same mistake twice.'

While everyone works for money in the final analysis, the reason they stay for the long term and give 110% is because of what goes with that. People need to feel satisfied, developed, encouraged and appreciated.

If all this sounds like a lot of hard work, retailers should remind themselves that talent will determine success. It is impossible to deliver a great experience, whether online or in-store, without the connection and contributions of a great team of people.

RETAIL GRAVEYARD *Comet, UK*

Four reasons why failure to invest added to the retailer's demise in 2012:

Reduced staff numbers

In a last-ditch effort to turn around the ailing store group, the owners revamped stores and introduced new marketing concepts, such as an eGift card and an interactive app. However, the staff count was reduced, even when this was potentially the chain's only possible source of differentiation.

Strong competitors

Comet was squeezed by strong competition from both internet retailers and supermarkets encroaching onto its territory of electrical goods. Online stores have the advantage of lower fixed costs, while supermarkets have greater buying power and a loyal customer base that visits regularly. Comet had no real point of difference.

Lack of training

Comet's main competitor, Dixons, invested millions in staff training, since the one thing bricks-and-mortar stores can do really well is offer face-to-face advice and guidance. The Comet team did not have the skills and product knowledge to create a relevant experience for customers.

Ill-equipped to meet changing tastes

Margins are notoriously thin on electrical goods. New products sell at a premium, then prices halve annually thereafter, meaning retailers have to sell double the volume to keep up. However, without investment in training and without working to understanding consumer behaviour, Comet's staff were ill-equipped to keep ahead.

Much of the focus here has been on bringing in great and talented people and then developing them. Of course, retail leaders frequently 'inherit' a team when they move from one company to another. I have certainly found myself in this situation on a number of occasions. The big question then is: How do you adapt the organisation to make sure everyone recognises and understands the culture you want?

People should always be the number one priority of any retailer. I have often been asked to join organisations with the corresponding enticement that the owner is about to spend £X million on refurbishing the store portfolio and updating the systems. These are all very important things. However, my response to this is, 'Great, but what are you doing about your people?'

There is always, quite understandably, great anxiety whenever there is a change at the top of any company. People naturally ask whether there will be change. I am always entirely honest when I join any retailer and say 'yes'. No job is entirely safe. We are all subject to the requirements of our stakeholders, whether we work for a public or private company. However, what I am most interested in is that everyone is involved in what I want to do and is passionate about succeeding.

There are always people who will put their heads down, hoping the current regime will soon pass. Equally, each new organisation I have joined will reveal a rich seam of tremendous talent. This is not to say the people who are keeping their heads down need to go. Often, it is simply a case of explaining what needs to be done and giving them encouragement. I use some of the training and development techniques I have described here and very often the less willing long-stayers turn into the stars of the bunch. I've worked with countless people who have blossomed into superstars. They just need to be given a chance. It is always possible to turn good people into great ones. It simply requires personal commitment and a management team determined to coach, support and inspire.

PROFESSIONAL VIEW
How to Be a Relevant Retailer

- Make the customer the focal point of all strategic and tactical execution decisions. This will help a retailer evolve quickly.
- Speed matters now more than ever.
- Empower and enable your team to be bold and fast – don't let the bureaucracy of the company and the size of the challenges slow you down.
- Find great people who are motivated; have a modern, youthful and relevant point of view; and are talented.

Pete Nordstrom
Co-president of Nordstrom, USA and Canada

Ultimately, the aim should always be that retail assistants feel pride in the place they work. Pride is a powerful motivator. The feeling that what you do is interesting, stimulating and worthwhile drives exceptional service, continued innovation and commitment. Think of companies famous for their exceptional service, such as Disney, Virgin and the John Lewis Partnership. None of these companies throw money around to motivate employees. Yet, each one has built a reputation through the pleasure their people take in working for the business.

Employees who love what they do and feel proud of where they work will speak openly and positively about it to colleagues, potential employees, customers and people in their community (airline bosses, please take note!). People who love what they do will do whatever is necessary to get the job done and get it right with enthusiasm and a smile.

Add all of these elements together and you'll create an energised, relevant workplace.

CHAPTER CHECKOUT

✓ People are the most important asset in a retail business. The right team can make or break companies. Listen to them: they will have valuable insights from the shop floor.

✓ I always describe passion as the human soul on fire – a good benchmark!

✓ Customers today want the people they deal with to be *passionate* about the products they sell. Store staff who understand and value the customer will always be winners.

✓ Time spent with your teams in stores is a valuable investment for CEOs and senior management teams.

Chapter eight

LEADERSHIP

The Saks Fifth Avenue's shoe floor caused a sensation when it opened in spring 2007. Both the mainstream and the fashion press talked breathlessly about the 30,000-square-foot department, which took up the entire eighth floor of the New York landmark, stocking three times more shoes and brands than anywhere else in town, or in fact anywhere. There were Jimmy Choo, Christian Dior, Gucci, Giorgio Armani, Valentino, Dolce & Gabbana, Jonathan Kelsey and Burberry. In fact, the department was so big, the US Postal Service even gave it its own zipcode: 10022-SHOE.

'Shoe heaven!' proclaimed one commentator.

'Dwarfs the collection of Imelda Marcos,' crowed another, referring to that most avid collector of shoes.

And, the pièce de résistance? Without a doubt that prize went to the exclusive Shoe Express elevator, which swiftly conveyed fashionistas up to the eighth floor, straight from the cosmetics and handbags department on the first.

The shoe floor, which opened a few months after I left my role as president of the Saks organisation, was an achievement. I can still well remember the moment when the idea was first mooted by Robert Wallstrom, who was at that time the vice president of the Fifth Avenue store.

I had visited the store one Saturday morning to check on things and do my customary walk-about, and I joined Rob for coffee in his office.

'We need more space for shoes,' he said, after I had greeted him.

I knew what he meant. This was one of our most popular departments, but we'd reached optimum capacity in terms of the number of brands, or indeed shoes, we could stock. Rob was right, we needed more space. A lot more space.

'What do you think about taking it to the eighth floor?' he said.

'What do you have in mind?' I prompted.

'Well, we've got a lot more space there,' he went on, speaking rapidly in his enthusiasm for the idea. 'We'd be able to increase footfall and stock more brands.'

I liked the idea a lot, but there were a number of potential barriers. The most obvious of those potential issues was how to get customers to go all the way up to the eighth floor in their quest for shoes. The offer would have to be pretty compelling to get sufficient traffic up to justify turning over the entire floor to footwear. The flipside of that was, if hundreds of people were beating a path skywards to reach the shoe department, wouldn't that jam up the elevators and prevent other customers from visiting Saks' other floors?

Even so, it was an exciting idea. Rob and I kicked around a few more and parted company agreeing to give it more consideration.

One of my first ports of call after that was to pick up the phone to chat to Rose Marie Bravo. While she had long since moved on to work her magic at Burberry, Rose Marie had served as president at Saks in the 1990s and knew the store and its customers better than anyone. Her response was very encouraging indeed and we discussed all the potential drawbacks in detail.

'Andrew, why don't you put an express elevator in?' she suggested. 'One that would go all the way from the first to the eight floor? That would solve a lot of problems, plus it would have a certain exclusivity about it which would be great for marketing.'

I loved the idea, sensing straight away it would be a winner.

I also chatted to Leonard Lauder, who was always a fantastic sounding board and who is closely tied to New York. If anyone had a finger on the pulse of what our potential customers would like, it would be him. He too was enormously encouraging and had some creative ideas on exciting new brands too.

Rob Wallstrom subsequently reported back from his research, which was similarly positive. Buoyed up by the findings, the team set about making this happen, with much flair and leadership coming from Terron Schaefer, who was then senior vice president of Creative and Marketing. The rest, as they say, is history, and the eighth-floor shoe department went on to be a roaring success and still is today.

The reason for telling this story is to illustrate what, to me, is one of the most crucial aspects of retail leadership: don't ever be afraid to be ambitious. In the quest for relevance, you will often need to do things that have never been done before. Indeed, it is imperative that you do so. The expression I use that so perfectly encapsulates this philosophy is 'go big or go home'.

PROFESSIONAL VIEW
How to Be a Relevant Retailer

- You need to understand your unique purpose – what do you do for your customers that keeps them coming back? The *what* you do will always evolve; the *why* is more important.
- Live with your customers: understand their lives and their digital world – what's new and interesting for them?
- Keep testing new ideas at scale – fail quickly and roll out winners quickly.
- Involve all of your colleagues with the challenge of constant evolution – what do they think customers want, and what could we try?

Sir Ian Cheshire
Chairman, Debenhams, International

Attaining and maintaining relevance will require some bold decisions. Take them! Work through your ideas, choose the strongest among them and then make them happen. The reason so many stores have fallen by the wayside is because they have tinkered at the edges, doing a little bit of this and a little of that.

When it comes to relevance, bold leadership is vital. It is the catalyst that brings all the other elements covered in this book together. Without effective leadership, there cannot be relevance. It won't ever happen 'by accident'. A strong leader will focus attention on what matters most.

Look at the stories behind the most relevant retailers you know today. Every single one has reached that position because the person at the top of that retail organisation made a big, brave decision. Or, perhaps even several of them. I featured Liberty as a 'Relevant Retailer' in chapter two, but it was not always this way. In fact, it spent some time in the doldrums before it was transformed by the vision of Ed Burstell, who took over at the iconic London store in 2008. Prior to this, a succession of people had run Liberty in an uninspiring, lacklustre fashion and, hardly surprisingly, it had limped along at the bottom of the department store pack. Retailers kept saying that the nooks and crannies at this quintessentially British store needed to be ironed out and brought into the modern world. Following the store's acquisition by BlueGem Capital in 2010, the retail community sat back and waited for the major construction project that would inevitably ensue. Except it didn't.

Ed was appalled at the idea of ditching what he saw as all the magic. The American retailer recognised what many of his British counterparts ignored, which was that tourists loved the mock-Tudor exterior and the plethora of little rooms dotted around the store that could only be accessed by characterful wooden stairs. The central London location, next door to iconic Carnaby Street, made the store an ideal candidate for a tourist-friendly strategy. Ed's big idea was all about putting the brand in front of a global audience. He wasn't interested in moving around the layout, knocking down doors and installing escalators; instead he thought big. He had a vision for Liberty and it had tremendous results.

RELEVANT RETAILER *Ira Neimark, Bergdoff Goodman, USA*

Five reasons why Ira Neimark's leadership skills transformed Bergdorf Goodman:

Focus on a big idea

When Ira Neimark took over as CEO at Bergdorf Goodman in 1975, he wanted to attract people with enough money to spend on the best the store could offer. Unfortunately, the store had a reputation for being old, dull, expensive and intimidating. His idea was to attract a young crowd with exciting and expensive goods – while retaining the intimidating atmosphere for exclusivity purposes.

Absolute stock control

Earlier in his career, Ira had learned the art of ruthlessly maintaining inventory while anticipating future sales. He ensured a constant turnover of hot designer items while discounting items that didn't sell by discretely merchandising them on off-price rails. Merchandise needs to keep moving.

Customers first

Ira's mantra was 'learn to know your customers' and he was fanatical about spending time in-store and speaking to the people who shopped there. He called it 'earning his MBWA degree', or Management By Walking Around. In his view, customers are 'always looking for something new to make their lives a bit more exciting, no matter what age or gender, in good times or bad.'

Understand the power of marketing and exclusivity

Aware of the buzz around French fashion at the time he became CEO, Ira persuaded Yves Saint Laurent, Dior and Givenchy to sell their couture exclusively at Bergdorf in the USA. He correctly predicted the flurry of media excitement that would greet their arrival and exploited it mercilessly, putting on shows at the Rockefeller ice-skating rink and Plaza's fountain, among other targeted activities

Think in the long term

Ira strongly believed that, while the finance department and shareholders are important, the direction a retailer takes should ultimately be up to the CEO. The person at the top has the full picture and truly understands the long-term implications. It's a gamble for those not on the front line, but it is one worth taking.

As the leadership stories from Liberty, the Saks shoe floor and indeed Ira Neimark so beautifully illustrate, the person at the head of a retail organisation needs to have a vision. This vision is the point of view that I described in chapter three. Our vision, or point of view, at Saks was to be a leader in fashion trends, offering our customers a comprehensive, yet carefully curated, selection of the very best brands in a stylish and exclusive environment.

When a retailer has a point of view, however ambitious, it reflects what the business is and can be. It is the task of a strong leader to ensure that the point of view is clearly understood and embraced by the whole team.

This core ideology embraces what a company stands for and why it exists. Wrapped up within that are aspirations for the future: what we aspire to become. How will we achieve this point of view? It is the task of a leader to ensure all future plans are measured against it. The leader is the glue that holds an organisation together as it expands, diversifies and develops. They keep the team focused and moving forward with unity and purpose. A clearly articulated point of view helps employees to understand the company's direction and their individual roles in getting it there. I have had the privilege of much international exposure in my career, working in leadership roles at some of the globe's best-known retail brands. However, whenever I start somewhere afresh, I always make sure I un-learn what I *think* I know about those retailers. I make no assumptions about their point of view or culture. I am more keen to see things are they really are.

Three words guide me during my first 30 days in any business: *look*, *learn* and *listen*. Whether it is new colleagues, senior staff, suppliers or business partners, I am interested in what *they* think the vision is for the business and how they are going about achieving it. The results of these observations are, as you might expect, highly illuminating. Generally, the more trouble a retailer is in, the more disparate the views are about how things are done. There will be various interpretations of the overall strategy (if one is noted at all) and just as many views on what needs to be done to achieve it.

When I joined Karstadt, which was my toughest assignment, the teams on the various shop floors seemed to have no idea at all about what the company stood for. For lack of any sort of direction, most staff appeared to assume that the strategy was simply to make money in whatever way presented itself. Thus, on my 30-day look, learn and listen tour, I was astonished to find out that the supposedly fashionable department store was selling vermin traps. These gruesome-looking devices would easily have been more at home among the buckets, brooms, detergents and poisons in a hardware shop.

'But they do sell,' said one of the Karstadt buying heads with a resigned shrug when I asked about them.

As the leader I had to ask the question: 'Do we want to be in the vermin trap business?'

The Karstadt example is extreme but illustrates just what can happen if there is no strong central point of view to follow. Inevitably, the team does their best with the hand they've been dealt but all sorts of horrible habits crop up. The chances of being relevant in an environment like this are zero.

It is a priority for any retail leader, whether they are new to the job or have been in place for years, to set and maintain a strong point of view. Then, they must make sure that everyone in the business understands it and knows the behaviour and attitude needed to achieve this overall vision or goal. A business that does not have everyone pulling in the same direction will eventually pull itself apart. These guiding principles show what is important in an organisation and what deserves attention, ranking everything a company does by its relevance to that aim. Thus, if a retailer is brand-driven and focused on its reputation and place in the market, the team should consider everything in terms of delighting the customer: How will our customers view this?

Leadership must clearly articulate and communicate the point of view and it needs to *mean* something. Those on the front line – sales staff or planners, buyers and merchandisers – don't want some vague waffle about 'pleasing customers' or 'being the best'. There need to be clearly defined, clearly stated objectives.

I once heard a lovely expression that sums this up perfectly and I now use it all the time: 'haze in the pulpit, fog in the pew'. In other words, if you are not 100% clear when preaching the message, the congregation is never going to get it. Clarity is crucial.

Leaders in retail today need to be fearless and used to being out of their comfort zone. It is a tough and challenging retail market place and CEOs need to create a culture of facing fear head-on.

When spreading the word about a retailer's point of view, one mechanism I have used successfully a number of times is to make it 'the way' – in other words, the way things are done around here. Over the years, I have worked through the Saks Way, the Holt Renfrew Way and the Woolworths Way. At Ted Baker, where I am a non-executive director, the brand has the Ted Way. Everything is about the Ted Way, from the way the team dress (Ted to Toe) to the way they communicate (Ted Talk).

The way sets out the types of behaviour I believe reflect the point of view and values of a retailer and what will best get us to where we need to be. It helps members of the team pull together in the same direction and, when new or unfamiliar situations occur for which no rules have been written, it helps store staff make a judgement and act consistently.

By way of an example, I have included an extract from the House of Fraser Way, which we delivered when I was group MD in the mid-1990s.

The House of Fraser Way

To our customers

We are the standards by which all other retailers are judged. Our service always makes our customers feel welcome, relaxed and attended to without being pressured. They know that with House of Fraser there are never any hidden problems, any small print which makes the service less attractive than it seems to be at first sight. Our customers know that they do not have to take a deep breath before asking us to help with a problem.

To our suppliers

We are tough, demanding, but fair. We do not tolerate second-rate offers and we are acknowledged as experts in our product fields, to whom no supplier would show second-rate products or incomplete ranges, nor would they expect us to agree to prices which are not the most competitive.

To our colleagues

We are all supportive professionals who are fully on top of our job brief, having the skills and knowledge to solve any problem in our area of responsibility and the enthusiasm to want to help each other in any way we can to improve the business's performance and profitability.

To our staff

We lead our staff, individually and as a team, using our skill, management ability and experience to catalyse the release of all their abilities in the service of the company. We take careful steps to ensure our staff know what we expect of them, ensure they have the right skills, knowledge and equipment to be confident that they can deliver what we want of them and, when they are successful, recognise that success. We value openness in communication and take steps to ensure that all staff are regularly briefed on the business and where they fit into it.

To our manager
We follow the manager's lead, using our enthusiasm, energy, talent and resources to support him/her in achieving his/her objectives. We think clearly, recognising the challenges our boss faces and ensuring that those things we have control over are performed to our utmost in support of him/her.

To our shareholders
We are a first-rate team who know where we are taking the company to increase the worth of their stake to the very best in retailing and giving them reliable and high-level dividends.

To the community at large
We are a good citizen, doing our part to stimulate commerce and create wealth in the locations where we and our suppliers operate providing jobs and careers.

I should say here that, while the House of Fraser Way was written down, which is what has enabled me to document it in its entirety here, this should never be as far as it goes. It would be a huge mistake to note down a retailer's values, distribute them to the senior team and leave it at that. Apart from anything else, it will never end well if 'how we do things around here' is dictated from senior levels just once and then forgotten about by one and all. No, everyone needs to know what a retailer stands for. It should be clearly communicated in everything the business does, all the time, again and again and again. Sticking up a sheet of values somewhere in the staff room, or publishing them on the company intranet, is no good at all.

Core values should be integrated into every process, from recruitment to performance management to promotions and rewards and even to dismissal. Right from the very first interview (actually, preferably in the job ad itself), people need to be constantly reminded of these core values and that they are the basis of the way the company works.

I have always found the way particularly useful when staff are brought in from other retailers. Often they might come from what I call a 'cocoon business', which is where things have always been highly structured, with a clear chain of command that leaves very little room for innovation or entrepreneurial thinking. The way is a useful guide to induct them into the business. I make a point of explaining that more individual thinking may be expected of them than they are used to, albeit within clearly defined parameters. The way gives guidance on how they act with customers, conduct meetings, write emails, communicate, buy merchandise and treat people – everything. If they can't respect that new way and embrace it, they might need to return to their cocoon.

Those at the top should never, ever miss an opportunity to reiterate the point of view. When I was group MD retail at Woolworths in South Africa, the CEO, Simon Susman, was a master at this. During every single meeting he was involved in, he would bring the Woolies Values into the discussion. Then, at various points during each meeting, he would take everyone back to the values once more. He never missed a chance to repeat what the business stood for. Simon would often appear unexpectedly in meetings and, invariably, he'd bring the discussion round to whether or not the matter in hand truly reflected the Woolies Values.

I vividly remember a range review that I was conducting with the chief merchant. Simon popped in and was concerned about the quality of the items in question. This was not unusual. If he felt the quality was below par for Woolies, he'd say so immediately. The buyer, who was new to the business, responded by saying the items were good value because they were available at the best price in the market.

'That is as may be,' Simon said with a smile. 'But does this meet our quality standards?'

Thanks to Simon's leadership, clarity and repetition, everyone in the entire organisation knew the Woolies Values. It was crystal clear what Woolies stood for. I can still remember them word for word today:

- Quality and style – always exceptional
- Value – always value with values
- Service – always customer first
- Innovation – create the difference

- Integrity – do what you say you will do: be transparent
- Energy – be passionate and deliver
- Sustainability – build for a better future

It should go without saying that, unless retail executives lead by example, the vision will very rapidly unravel. If there is a disconnect, it will very quickly be uncovered. If the management tier loudly trumpets its core value as one of 'open collaboration' yet in practice the opinions of colleagues are very quickly shot down in flames, things will very quickly fall apart. Unsurprisingly, the team will soon hold back from voicing an opinion or making any effort to collaborate.

Another thing that is very much worth noting here is the need for sustainability, which is something that should very much be led from the top of an organisation. There is widespread awareness of the environmental and social challenges of our time and any retailer that chooses to ignore these issues does so at its peril. Continuing with the story of Woolworths South Africa, the retailer has always been aware of its responsibilities and has rightly been named the World Retail Congress's Responsible Retailer of the Year on a number of occasions.

To Woolworths, being a sustainable retailer means not only minimising its impact but also positively contributing to the livelihoods of people within the organisation and to the wellbeing of its customers, people within its supply chain and the environment. Woolworths' Good Business Journey is its strategy to improve upon the ethical standards employed in relation to people and animals within the company's supply chain. The Good Business Journey's eight focus areas are:

1. water;
2. waste management;
3. energy and climate change;
4. sustainable farming;
5. transformation;
6. social development;
7. health and wellness;
8. ethical sourcing.

The retailer works directly with the majority of its producers to manage, monitor and transform environmental performance through programmes such as Farming for the Future, tackling areas such as sustainable pesticide and fertiliser application, efficient irrigation and soil conservation.

During my tenure there, we spent a lot of time working through the Woolworths Trust to raise and disperse funds to causes that were very close to our hearts. One of my favourite examples was EduPlant, which helps schools in disadvantaged communities to create gardens to grow fruit, vegetables, herbs and medicinal plants for the community. Supporting such initiatives is just one way that Woolworths presents a more modern image of the future to its customers, by associating itself with the ideas, information and causes they care about. At the same time, Woolworths' support of EduPlant strengthened the relationship we had with the parents of the children whose schools were helped; the parents viewed the Woolworths brand as trustworthy and respectful. We always encouraged all employees to embody the Good Business Journey by developing fundraising efforts and initiatives in their local communities.

Woolworths, South Africa -- EduPlant sustainability project

RETAIL GRAVEYARD *Blockbuster, UK*

Five reasons why management's failure to keep up with a changing market called time on Blockbuster:

Too slow to adapt

While Blockbuster boasted thousands of retail outlets for video rental, millions of films and an efficient service, there was a flaw in its strategy: it was too slow to adapt to changes in the market.

Customer-unfriendly proposition

Revenues depended on charging customers fees for returning films late. Without penalising patrons, Blockbuster couldn't make a profit. It was vulnerable to internet start-ups that let customers keep a video for as long as they wanted.

Underestimated rivals

Blockbuster was slow to invest in a digital platform, even when it became very apparent that competitors such as Netflix and Redbox were stealing market share. Management turned down flat an approach from Netflix, which offered to pool resources.

Divided board, with a focus on short-term profitability

CEO John Antico did finally persuade the board to change direction, abolishing late fees and investing in digital, in his 'Total Access' strategy, but not everyone in the company was convinced thanks to the high costs of implementing the changes. Activist investors questioned the CEO's strategy and he was ousted in a compensation dispute.

Strategy reversal

Antico's successor reversed the Total Access strategy in order to increase profitability. Blockbuster went bankrupt five years later.

Leadership is not easy. Indeed, in the current, challenging retail environment, it is more difficult than ever.

I have listed below five key traits I feel a successful leader needs in the retail market today. Some of the attributes may seem unnatural, even impossible at first glance. Yet, to successfully lead an organisation to relevance, this is the level of leadership required.

The five often unnatural acts of the true leader of a relevant retailer are:

1. Refuse to be a prisoner of experience
Don't stick to the 'safe' option because it has always worked in the past. Relevant retailers are always trying something new.

2. Develop right versus right decision making – not right versus wrong
Achieving relevance will require some tough decisions. Leaders shouldn't get bogged down with making the 'right' or 'wrong' choices. Instead, look at your role as optimising the choice between trade-offs to achieve a given objective. You'll always have to give up one thing to get another – accept it. In fact, embrace it.

3. Trust before it is earned
As Ernest Hemingway once said, 'The way to make people trust-worthy is to trust them'.[19] Trust your team from the off. It improves communication and the flow of ideas.

4. Coach and teach rather than lead and inspire
Don't become too obsessed by your own abilities and achievements. Encourage others to find success, mentor them in achieving more than they believed they could and together you will all find yourselves being more innovative and creative.

5. Challenge conventional wisdom
Always!

---

19 *Ernest Hemingway Selected Letters 1917–1961*, edited by Carlos Baker, Scribner's, 1981

Leadership

To become truly relevant, it is imperative that a retailer stands for something. In my view, you either stand for something or you stand for nothing.

Leading and inspiring people are challenging whatever business you are in. I have spent a career in six countries over two hemispheres, deeply involved in the development of talent within the retail industry. I have had the pleasure of working with many of the retail leaders of today as they rose to the top. After observing them in action and analysing my own experiences, there is no question in my mind that maximising the development of your talent is key to realising the full potential of any retailer. I am sure to always hire people with passion for what they do and then listen to them and give them the space to make enlightened risks and make mistakes (and, most importantly, to learn from them quickly). I also prioritise continuously developing the most talented people and encouraging and inspiring them through great leadership. This enables me to be innovative in the ways I expose them to ideas and challenge their thinking.

The members of a retail team will, quite rightly, have high expectations of their leader. The fact that he or she must make good decisions is a given, but they'll also be judging the leader (and therefore making up their minds whether to give their all) on the basis of the leader's credibility, their ability to interact at all levels, the information they provide and the effort they put into motivating those around them.

To be relevant and move a retail business from good to great, you need relevant leaders who inspire their team to do extraordinary things. They need to be passionate, talented and empowered to do what they do best. It doesn't matter if they make mistakes. Getting the leadership role right will make the difference between success and failure. Modern and dynamic retail businesses need to recruit and nurture leaders who are willing to take enlightened risks, to innovate and to 'execute with excellence' at every level of the organisation. Those leaders will, in turn, recruit a senior team that will ruthlessly implement strategies and operational plans, encouraging those below them to exceed expectations and be remarkable.

Retail, as an industry, is blessed with some extraordinary talent at the top, and I have mentioned many people I admire in this book. There are numerous merchants with real vision who have transformed stores and store groups into entirely different, enticing propositions. There is, however, always room for more talent.

CHAPTER CHECKOUT

✓ When starting a new assignment or job, there are three key words to keep in mind during the first 30 days: look, listen and learn.

✓ Create a clear and compelling vision of the future centred around your customers.

✓ Relentlessly keep everyone aligned and invest heavily in your talent. Listen to them and give them the space to take enlightened risks and to make mistakes and learn from them quickly.

✓ Always be bold with your ideas – go big or go home.

Chapter nine

RETAIL MARKETING –A VISUAL TREAT

I joined Holt Renfrew in the winter of 1998, and it was immediately apparent the 165-year-old store group was showing signs of becoming irrelevant. While everyone was extremely fond of the stores that made up this grand speciality store chain, many customers were bored with it as it had not moved as quickly as its US counterparts. Its customers were visiting it less and less and becoming increasingly infrequent with their purchases. The vision of my new team was to deliver a holistic, exciting customer experience and to reinvent Holts as one of the most vibrant and talked-about retail businesses in the world. I have described much about how we did this throughout this book. However, as everyone knows, one can merchandise a store full of the most chic goods in the world, but, if prospective customers don't have a clue the goods are there, there is little point in doing so. After all the hard

Holt Renfrew, Toronto – Viva Italia gala event

work building the foundations, I needed a fantastic, high-profile marketing campaign to tell Canada's fashion customers that Holts was now *the* place to be.

One of the many answers we came up with was *Viva Italia*.

Viva Italia was a three-week spectacular merchandise and marketing campaign that was as enormous as it was extravagant. This incredible piece of theatre celebrated all things Italian, from artisanal food to wine to fashion and of course homewares. The focus of the event was to wake up Canada with a one-of-a-kind retail extravaganza that positioned Holt Renfrew at the forefront of North American retailing.

Naturally, we began our campaign by going straight after sponsors from the best-known Italian fashion houses, such as Armani and Dolce & Gabbana. We persuaded designers such as Roberto Cavalli and James Ferragamo to make personal appearances at one of the many gala evenings that were planned. We managed to talk Sophia Loren into joining in with the celebrations as Patron of Honour.

From the brief account I have given here, this might all sound rather easy. I can assure you it wasn't. To begin with, no one was at all sure they wanted to be involved with this event. However, my team would not take no for an answer and I actively encouraged the development of a mindset that found 'no' completely unacceptable.

I had five golden rules for this project.

The first rule was that we needed to give ourselves enough time to complete the planning of the promotion. I didn't want to launch the event unless it was 100% ready. If we were going to announce that we had a major event in the works, we had better appear with something that would take our customers' collective breath away. This is why we began developing links and relationships *two years* before the actual *Viva Italia* event. Whether it was the Italian government, brands or designers, we were knocking on doors a long, long time before the launch. Meanwhile, while I was busily drumming up enthusiasm from potential contributors, I was also banging the drum equally hard back at home. I never once missed an opportunity to extol the benefits of this promotion to our team and whip up the fervour around it. This was my second rule: I needed a strong, committed team who were fully supportive of the new vision and the steps we were taking to realise it.

As time moved on, I became aware of a halo effect. My team were so excited and enthusiastic about being involved that they talked about the event to anyone who would listen. Outsiders couldn't help being drawn into the new buzz around Holts: after all, everyone loves newness. We found the planning of *Viva Italia* started to play an important part in attracting new, high-calibre staff. We were already beginning to be *the* place to be.

Without support from the core team, it would have been virtually impossible to adhere to my third rule: avoid obstacles. As my 'no nos' rule showed, I was pretty single-minded about the success of *Viva Italia*. Once everyone got what I was trying to do, we reached the stage where I could say to the team, 'This is how it has to be – *you find a solution*. Find me someone who can walk through a wall.'

And, guess what? They invariably managed to do just that.

Of course, monumental promotions like this mean huge budgets. This inevitably puts the people with the ideas on a collision course with the people who hold the purse strings. However, I've always been a big believer that 'budget restraints' are all too often used as an excuse. People hide behind financial projections and spreadsheets. I wasn't going to let this hold me back. The solution that satisfies all parties (even the CFO) is to be fully prepared and have a robust back-up plan, because that will get barriers to crumble. For an event like this, our big wall-breaker was sponsorship. Thus, a focus on amassing plenty of sponsors was my fourth golden rule. For *Viva Italia*, we managed to get sponsorship from suppliers, American Express and even the Italian government. This took a lot of the financial pressure off. Signing up some of the bigger names took a fair amount of self-belief as well as a carefully documented and calculated plan. It also took a little bit of chutzpah, but we did it.

As I said to the team at the time: 'We negotiated with major suppliers, who had heard it all before; we negotiated with the credit card supplier, who had heard it all before; and we negotiated with the Italian government, who had never heard it before, and we succeeded! Not bad for a 12-store speciality group in Canada.'

My fifth rule, perhaps illogically, was to start with the 'end in mind'. In other words, imagine what it is that you want the event to be like. Paint such a wonderful picture with your words that people can't help but say 'wow' when you explain it to them. They can barely visualise that such a thing could

Retail marketing – a visual treat

Holt Renfrew, Toronto – Viva Italia gala event

happen and yet you make them believe it is possible. Then you work out how to make it happen!

We did make it happen, too. The *Viva Italia* promotion was one of the most successful events I was ever involved in. Holt Renfrew achieved record sales as a result and increased its store traffic by 20%, with most of these people going on to become regular customers because they saw how we'd transformed their once down-at-heel store and loved it. The event was a hit in the press too: Holts secured domestic and international media coverage worth more than $7 million. It completely changed the way customers thought about Holt Renfrew, which was, of course, completely the point.

As I so often say: if you think small, you'll deliver small. The *Viva Italia* idea was big, but it did what it set out to do. The glitz and glamour woke up the Canadian public and in the process completely redefined what Holt Renfrew stood for. It was an event that was much appreciated by the Italians too. The President of the Italian Republic awarded me the *Grande Ufficiale Ordine al Merito della Repubblica Italiana*, one of the highest civilian awards. I didn't do it for the gong, but it was a lovely touch and a real honour for myself and the team.

PROFESSIONAL VIEW
How to Be a Relevant Retailer

- Differentiate. It was ever thus, but, if there is not something you have that flows against the tide, that sets you apart and that it is hard for others to match, you will fail. In the modern retail environment, 'generic' will kill you.

- Look forward and back. Being evangelical about future technology, new retail models and the latest consumer thinking can be just as dangerous as being a fully-paid-up member of the retail 'flat Earth society' ('ecommerce will never catch on' or 'the new competition aren't relevant'!). Have a sense of history, be a fast follower and go for a few key strategic 'jokers'. It's the fusion of the three that counts.

- Have a vision. I am amazed how many retailers just fall back on low-level pragmatism. Have a clear-eyed view of where you want to get to: a true aspiration that will inspire both your home team and your customers. Aiming low becomes self-fulfilling.

- It's all about the customer. Don't be seduced by a hundred 'plumbing' projects. Yes, you need good platforms, logistics, IT core development and financial processes. But, if they become an all-consuming focus, inevitably the top line does not move, and investment and cash dry up. A single-minded view on consumer proposition must lead at all times.

Peter Ruis
CEO, Jigsaw, International

Holts is not the only retailer to understand the marketing power of big promotions like this. Indeed, Selfridges is the absolute master of the art. Each year it holds a number of big, retail-theatre-style campaigns. One of the first to kick this off was its iconic £1 million Bollywood promotion in 2002. Mehndi body painting and Hindi music were everywhere throughout the Oxford Street flagship store, which was over-hung with billowing red and yellow drapes. Customers supped on *pani-puri* and were queuing for signed copies of Bollywood movies. The sense of exotic glamour was palpable. Then there was the unforgettable Body Craze promotion, which saw American artist Spencer Tunick lead 500 naked people through Selfridges one morning. The spectacle was complemented by live dance acts and acrobatic performances, catwalk makeovers and free consultations from experts on non-cosmetic surgery such as Botox. Another notable Selfridges first was The Beauty Project, which involved a huge teaser wrap around the store, which was unveiled to reveal dramatic window displays posing various questions about beauty. The promotion, intended to be a celebration of beauty in all its forms, included numerous glitzy events, films and discussions, all themed around exploring the subjective definitions of beauty.

One of the most eye-catching events at Selfridges was launched in the spring of 2016. EveryBody introduced Selfridges' new Body Studio, which sells lingerie, loungewear, sleepwear, hosiery and athleisure collections in one location in the Oxford Street store. As part of the opening, Selfridges celebrated the body and the joy of movement, and also explored wellbeing. It was a brilliantly executed festival of beauty.

Do these events sell more merchandise? You bet they do! They are what make Selfridges one of the most relevant retail destinations in the world. It is fresh, exciting, vibrant and constantly changing. That is what clever marketing can do.

Selfridges, London – The Body Studio

Big promotional events give people a reason to go to a store. Sure, many of the products that are sold there can be bought elsewhere, or even online, but then you'd miss out on all the fun. These experiences bring a retail brand to life and motivate the customer to take action and visit the store. Once there, they're reminded of how it is even better than how they remembered it to be.

Of course, there is so much more to marketing than eye-catching, one-off promotions. Indeed, it's a huge and diverse discipline today that employs all sorts of different tactics to capture the imagination and interest of customers. Retailers can 'speak' to people in their homes via their TVs, PCs or mobile devices. They can also take their messages outside, so customers are constantly assailed while out and about via posters, video advertising boards, leaflets, push notifications and texts. Vloggers can be hired to reach out to their armies of Twitter and Instagram followers, speaking directly to 6 or 7 million people at a time about your store. Alternatively, in an age when the cult of the celebrity rules, well-known names can be paid (top dollar) to sprinkle on the magic of their personal endorsement. Stores can welcome individual customers at the exact moment they walk through the doors, giving them offers on products relevant to what they've bought before. And all of this is before you get to the exciting promotion and technology gizmos that can be used in-store to keep customers entertained.

It is all a far cry from the time in years gone past when, other than in-store events, retailers mainly relied on newspaper and magazine ads to get their brand out there. Some chains, though not many, also relied on leaflet drops, which invariably offered big discounts, loudly flagged up by ubiquitous large red lettering.

CROWD PLEASER *Rihanna and River Island, International*

Rihanna's edgy, flirtatious, eclectic collections for River Island helped to increase sales by more than 4%. However, the year-long celebrity collaboration in 2013 was not just about selling more fashion. It was designed to boost the fashion chain's reputation on the international stage, just as it was opening a series of new stores abroad in locations such as South Africa, Sweden, Malta, Estonia and the Philippines. The singer's global appeal was just what River Island needed to support its strategy to build the business through multiple channels and markets. Rihanna backed the campaign by personally modelling her own collections, which incorporated a mix of urban sports luxe and city chic. Not surprisingly, the idea was a huge hit with fashion fans.

We've come a long way in marketing terms, right?

Except have we? Scratch below the surface and it begins to become apparent that our marketing efforts are not always quite as sophisticated as they initially appear.

Take a look at your email inbox. I don't need to be a psychic to predict that you probably have dozens and dozens of emails in there, all sent by retailers. You may have only ever bought one thing from some of them. It could even have been months if not years ago that you last visited them. Yet, the email appears to blissfully ignore that fact as it breathlessly invites you to visit once more. Of course, you'll only know about that breathless invitation if you are in the habit of making the effort to actually open these missives. Most people I know simply highlight all these junk emails and press the delete button. And who can blame them? Apart from the sheer mind-numbing quantity of them, most aren't even relevant. A friend of mine recently told me she is still receiving messages from a well-known retailer of toddlers' clothing even though her two children are now teenagers. She bought from there once and yet the brand seems to feel that, like Peter Pan, all children never grow up. One can only conclude that, far from being in a sophisticated new world, we are not a great deal further on from the days of leaflet drops through our letterboxes. The only difference is, we get many, many more emails than we ever got leaflets. The explanation for this is that leaflets are/ were expensive to produce while millions of emails can be sent at the click of a mouse – but this is not sufficient justification for indiscriminate use. There is far too much noise email-wise, and moreover it is not well enough targeted and is mostly completely irrelevant to all concerned.

Looking around, this daily flurry of emails is not the only area in which retailers are in danger of making themselves completely irrelevant. Or worse. One of the marketing tools being used far too much – and as a bit of a blunt instrument – is price. Increasingly desperate waves of email communications now invariably offer 20% off. Another friend recently remarked to me that she never, ever shops full price at a high-profile mid-market fashion and homewares retailer. 'I just wait until I get one of those 20% off emails,' she said. 'I know they are always in my inbox, or will turn up soon.'

It is a difficult conundrum for the retail industry. In the age of Amazon, whose spiders sweep the market every few seconds to see how rival retailers are pricing products and then almost immediately lower Amazon's prices to stay below them, what is a retailer to do? Except in the case of luxury goods, where the manufacturer or brand has a lot of control over distribution (and thus price), there seems to be no easy solution to combat this problem. Even so, a solution must be found. Price should never be the marketing battleground for any retailer (unless it is a discounter and that is its unique selling point) and it is absolutely not a basis on which to build relevance.

Another marketing tool that is being completely mismanaged is loyalty schemes. These electronic cards were first introduced in 1982 and we all ended up with wallets full of the things. The UK loyalty market has become one of the most significant in the world and the schemes are still hugely popular among American store groups too. In recent years, many retailers have started to switch to loyalty apps, but I wonder whether we have all missed the point a little as we plough on with the concept.

While loyalty and rewards schemes seemed like a very charming idea when they were first launched, since they gave regular customers an incentive to go on shopping with a particular retailer, there was another, more pertinent reason for introducing them. Back then, in the pre-internet days, retailers knew very, very little about their customers. Getting them to sign up to a loyalty scheme was a perfect way to get them to give up loads of personal details that could, in turn, be used to market to them in a more appropriate way. We've all heard the story about the frequent nappy buyers who are sent offers on beer based on the grounds that with young children around there won't be much going out for a while!

Don't get me wrong, there is still very much a place for loyalty cards and apps. The customer expects and appreciates the instant gratification of points-based gift vouchers or rewards, the latter of which can be anything from a cup of coffee to an exclusive preview invitation to free gift wrapping for a special occasion. Today, though, there is no need for retailers to put the priority on such devices to gather personal data. Retailers are drowning under the sheer quantity of information they have about their customers. In fact, they have so much they don't even know what to do with it (and I will come to this). And, if they need any more, they can ask for it. No one bats an eyelid at being asked to hand over personal details when they check out. In a physical store, many customers are cooperative when it comes to sharing their email addresses. Online, they can be persuaded to part with even more as they pay for their goods. As this is the case, isn't it time the whole scheme had a revamp?

In today's super-competitive, customer-centric landscape, building loyalty and increasing brand recognition are essential. Modern capabilities around customer data management and unified customer identities are giving smart retailers the ability to devise more sophisticated and creative loyalty programmes because they have a better understanding of their customer base. The omnichannel trading philosophy adds new opportunities for retailers to personalise customer loyalty programmes to their own geographies.

Retailers can draw from the extensive information they've already gathered about behaviours and create smarter loyalty programmes that are accessible across all channels. I personally love the Harvey Nichols loyalty app for its customer-friendly appeal, and it has been remarkably successful and very popular with customers.

RETAIL GRAVEYARD *Banana Republic, UK*

Five reasons why Banana Republic UK did not capture the imagination:

Lacklustre presence

American workwear brand Banana Republic closed all eight of its UK stores in 2016 after just eight years in the market. It arrived to great fanfare, on the eve of the global financial crisis, but the slightly uninspiring appearance of the stores failed to capture the attention of UK shoppers, resulting in correspondingly lacklustre sales.

Changing market preferences

The financial crisis markedly changed the shopping preferences of UK customers, who became value hunters, either turning to discount stores or waiting for sales to make purchases. Banana Republic UK seemed unaware of this and did not appear to change its strategy in any way.

Presence too small to make an impact

Intense competition from chains such as Zara and H&M made it challenging for any chain with only a handful of stores. Banana Republic UK's presence on the high street and low-key marketing meant it was barely noticeable.

Slow to update trends

Banana Republic UK's product offering stayed largely the same. It certainly failed to compete quickly enough with changing fashions and tastes, soon acquiring a tired, dated feel. Fashion commentators openly said it was staid, boring and a little old fashioned.

Not value for money

The prices were felt to be high, certainly in comparison with the retailer's competitors, which were generally believed to offer better value for money.

If one accepts that retail marketing efforts need to be more refined in order to be as relevant as possible to the modern customer, the starting point must surely be with that customer. Retailers need to understand who their customers are. Really understand.

I've worked with many retailers over the years and invariably they will all say, very earnestly, that they know exactly who their customer is thanks to those reams of information they've gathered over the years. Very often they will list all her personality traits, likes and dislikes and, occasionally, even give her an affectionate name.

'Oh, she's a Jane,' they'll say, with some certainty.

Then they'll add that Jane likes this or likes that, all to demonstrate that they are fully cognisant of and in line with their customers' preferences.

It is only when I dig deeper, though, that I discover Jane is just 20% of their customer base. Yes, they have customers with all these carefully noted attributes, but many other people with entirely different views and tastes are passing through their doors and, it appears, going completely unnoticed. This must surely be part of the reason that so much marketing activity is wasted. Everyone is focused on Jane, while Saj, Sarah and Jo are either ignored or targeted with completely wasted, off-target communications.

All being well, there might be hundreds of different customers visiting a store each day. To be relevant, we need to be far more aware of who *all* of these people are. Yes, we need to know about our core customer, the Janes of this world, but if you dig deeper you will discover there are many types of important customer. Accurate segmentation of the market should be the starting point for any marketing campaign. To explain how this might work, let me use the example of Woolworths in South Africa. When I joined the company in 2006, it was clear that we needed a customer segmentation programme. For those who don't know it very well, Woolworths is similar to the UK's M&S chain – just more modern. It has a premium food offering that is the best in South Africa and a mid-market clothing range that its customers know and trust. Woolworths is the type of brand that resonates with a large section of the population. Indeed, there are few people in South Africa who don't have an opinion about it. However, when I joined, not all of those opinions were entirely positive. When asked, some customers responded, 'Woolies' clothes are too basic for me' or 'Woolies' food is too expensive for me'.

The challenge for us was how to retain our loyal customer base while also forging new links for new customers to shop at Woolworths. We decided upon a programme to identify our customers, existing and potential, and to explore what issues such as affordability, quality, value for money and fashion credentials meant to each one. In short, we wanted to be able to:

- know who our customers were;
- understand their needs and wants;
- predict what they were likely to want next;
- measure what worked effectively and refine it accordingly.

My preferred method of customer segmentation is to use a nine-box grid, something I have introduced into Woolworths and several other retailers over the past 30 years. As with any such graphic representation, there are two axes, the vertical and the horizontal. The definitions can change depending upon the circumstances. So you might have 'Good', 'Better' and 'Best' along the vertical, or 'Classic', 'Modern' and 'Contemporary'. The vertical and horizontal grids might equally well divide the customers up by sex, age, whether they have kids, or product preference (for example, clothing, home or basics). It can also work as a six-box grid, depending on the complexity of the market.

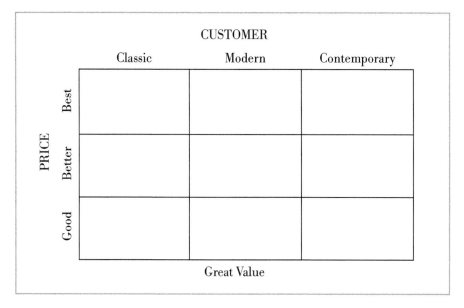

Figure 3. Nine-box grid

The nine-box grid is a very powerful information tool. It is populated with internal brands and labels which gives a very accurate snap shot/ depiction of the customer base, which ranges from the highly valuable 'Premium Taste' segment (who shop the exclusive brands, store brands and branded premium beauty) to 'Modern Basics' (which encompasses lower-spending customers who are far less engaged with the brand). Once a customer base has been clearly defined in this way, there are few questions that can be posed where it is not possible to provide a clear, segmented view of the answer.

The grid also provides a base point to conduct further detailed research into each segment to understand more about why the individual customers behave in the way they do. Plus, we can discover:

- the size and potential value of each segment and its importance to each category;
- the size and value of the segment in the market as a whole and our market share and potential market share;
- the most important competitors in each segment, including their strengths and weaknesses;
- customer attitudes to the brand, lifestyle, quality and value offered by the retailer.

Once a retailer has conducted an exercise like this, it is possible to more accurately develop and refine a strategy to communicate effectively with customers. Customers in each segment can be 'spoken to' in a way they understand and respond to, rather than simply sending the same message to everyone in an extremely wasteful scattergun approach. In the case of Woolworths, not only were we able to refine our ranges to suit the individual segments but we could also market to them on a segmented basis, using the precise customer data we now had. Knowing more about each individual allowed us to shape our communications better. We were also able to refine our loyalty programme so it became more meaningful, giving individual customers relevant, timely offers and rewards.

Woolworths' nine-box grid gave direction, and the new focus that came out of it was hugely successful. I'm happy to say that it became ingrained into the store group's psyche too. When I left, I was presented with a tray made up of a kaleidoscope of my nine-box grid.

'You were crazy on that nine-box grid,' the chairman, Buddy Hawton, joked. 'But you were entirely right. It gave us a consistent point of view.'

CROWD PLEASER *Hema, Europe*

The Dutch retailer Hema wanted to dramatically increase its market share of back-to-school stationery as one of its key competitors had gone into insolvency. In the summer of 2016, Hema launched a Back to School campaign to reach 12–18-year-olds. The store couldn't use traditional media, since this would have had no traction with the target group, and instead zoomed into the online world. Working on the premise that teens are developing their own identity and constantly looking for ways to establish themselves in the world, the main thrust of the campaign was around an offer of a complete range of school material that could be customised to a teen's personal style. Teens were alerted to it via online content, in particular vloggers, Snapchat and social media posts. Social influencers and vloggers were crucial to the promotion, reaching hundreds of thousands of members of the target group with relevant content. Sales of products endorsed on vlogs went up by 70%, and many top-voted products sold out in days. To complement the campaign, 'teen hangouts' were created in-store, with Wi-Fi, music and comfortable couches.

Hema, Netherlands – Giving tips on how to become vloggers

RELEVANT RETAILER *John Lewis, International*

Five ways in which John Lewis creates a powerful Christmas marketing message year after year:

Consistent quality

The John Lewis Christmas ad has become *the* signal that the festive season is underway. Regular and reliable as clockwork, it kick-starts the festivities and year after year it delivers just the right mix of powerful emotion and joy, playing on the population's heartstrings just at the moment when they are most susceptible.

Massive build-up

The John Lewis ad doesn't just arrive on our small screens. In the weeks that run up to its launch, the UK department store chain skilfully orchestrates the build-up like the release of a major blockbuster. Social media begins to buzz in anticipation at each new snippet that is carefully allowed out. The campaign is self-perpetuating because everyone has an opinion and is keen to share it online. The culmination is the release of the advert on Twitter.

Celebrity links

Each year, the chain has successfully chosen an up-and-coming music celebrity to sing the cover song for their ad. Past singers have included Ellie Goulding, just after she won the Critics' Choice Award at the Brits, and also Lily Allen, Gabrielle Aplin and Tom Odell. Very often, the ad cover songs go straight to the top of the charts following the first screening.

Not a blatant sales pitch

The ads don't feature a line-up of enticing products that you might like to buy for loved ones. They focus on drawing the audience in with something compelling that reflects John Lewis' point of view.

Cute kids and animals

Whoever said never work with children or animals never told the John Lewis marketing team. The department store group invariably features cute kids and animals in its campaign. And why not? Most of the popular videos on the internet do just that, and if you can't beat them, join them. It clearly works.

As I have said repeatedly, point of view is what a retailer needs, and this is crucial in a retailer's marketing efforts. If you don't know your customer, it is impossible to have a point of view and therefore a relationship with them. It is rather like shooting at a target with a shotgun. Yes, you will hit it, but you'll waste a lot of energy. What you need is a rifle, or even better a laser gun.

As well as more careful targeting, something I believe every retailer could do a lot better is to be consistent. In this wonderful world of omnichannel retail, the area that is often lagging behind is customer communication. There seems to be hostility between the various selling channels, which often translates into each department doing its own thing. This single-mindedness doesn't just produce mixed, confusing marketing messages – it can also impact the bottom line. Let me give you a real-life example. A good friend bought a coat from a well-known department store as a Christmas present for her mother-in-law. She paid full price and was completely happy with her purchase. That very evening, she received an email from the same store detailing all of its pre-Christmas offers. My friend could barely believe it when she saw her mother-in-law's coat was now 30% off. What did she do? The very next day, she returned the coat (which was still being sold at full price in-store), received a refund and then bought the same coat online, from the same store, at a discount. Joined-up marketing? I don't think so. Plus, my friend was left scratching her head and with a pretty poor impression of this particular store.

PROFESSIONAL VIEW
How to Be a Relevant Retailer

- Channels – like water down a hill, your customer will always find the fastest, most convenient and cheapest way to shop.
- Innovation – customers will always desire new and exciting products.
- Values – you will stay relevant if you deliver the best price or the best added value in your proposition.
- People – never lose sight of the importance of your people in making service and customer experience your differentiator.

Tony De Nunzio
Chairman, Pets at Home, UK

In marketing, we can never forget the basics either. It's not only about direct communication with the customer, promotions and offers. It should be about what they find when they walk through the doors. The look and feel of a store is crucial, particularly as a tool to combat the continual and growing competition from online.

I am often asked about how important visual merchandising is and I always say it should be an absolute priority. Creative presentation of in-store merchandise is essential. In a fashion area, for example, exceptional standards of mannequin dressing and great lighting are crucial to highlight products effectively. If I only had a limited budget for store renovation, I would focus this all into lighting and visual merchandise to present the merchandise to the customer in the most attractive way possible. I would also prioritise talented staff who understand visual standards and coordination.

Retailers must put all their efforts into assailing every sense of the human body. Stores should be a source of visual delight and discovery at every turn, with every square foot of the layout planned and executed to perfection. The aroma of the store should be just right, whether it is of delicate vanilla, coffee or a fine fragrance that is being launched. Similarly, the music should not be intrusive, yet it should complement the point of view that has been taken. Nothing can simply be left to chance.

Video should be an important part of the marketing mix too. Better internet speeds, widespread free Wi-Fi and cheaper data plans are making watching online videos less challenging, whether in-store or at home. For marketers there is a golden opportunity to introduce videos to add value to the customer experience. Just remember: customers do not live in a vacuum, so if you are not on top of your game your competitor will pip you to the post.

PROFESSIONAL VIEW
How to Be a Relevant Retailer

- Unleash the digital talent in your organisation across all functional areas – where do your customers shop, hang out and spend their money? What does that mean for your future customer offer?
- Push the boundaries on innovation – look to 'future proof' your investments.
- Don't overcomplicate your offer – keep it simple and intuitive.
- Embrace challenge and personality within your team.

Stacey Cartwright
CEO, Harvey Nichols Group, International

Relevant retailers need to act like magnets to attract customers, and that means paying the utmost attention to these basics. I often correct retailers who advise me that they need to *drive* more traffic into their stores. Retail stores and websites must become magnets to *attract* and draw the customer into the business. I have a strong point of view on this.

My top picks for visual merchandising across the globe would be Selfridges in London and Lane Crawford in Hong Kong. Each store has a knack of constantly looking like it is of the moment and at the leading edge, though each one does so in an entirely different way. This is not to forget visual impact from the value brands, and great examples of high visual merchandising standards can be seen at Uniqlo's flagship store on Fifth Avenue, New York, and Primark in Madrid.

Special mention should go to the Paris-based retailer Merci, an innovative concept store that is a charming combination of urban loft, library and garden café. The sensory impression is one that speaks to customers' desire for discovery, tranquillity, luxury and philanthropy.

The impact of a store should extend to every aspect of the shopping experience too, however apparently incidental. In the past it was the job of an on-floor sales person to greet the customer and encourage them to buy a product or service. Today, there are so many more opportunities and technologies available to appeal to a customer visually at all stages of the shopping expedition, whether online or in-store.

Plus, of course, there is the big-theatre aspect. I opened this chapter talking about big events, but this sort of activity should also be supported by regular smaller events. Stores should 'own' occasions such as Mother's Day, Father's Day and Valentine's Day. While I was at Holts, we did a special Valentine's Day pack containing half a bottle of champagne, sexy underwear, chocolate body paint and a cheeky card. The customers loved it.

Where there aren't specific days or events, you can create your own. One year, my marketing team promoted 'grandparent survival kits' for the school holidays. We reasoned that many grandparents look after children during the summer, so it might work well to create a promotion around this. We scoured the store for slow-selling lines and created a 'dress-up' box of hats, shirts and coats, and various other imaginative things to do. It was a huge success.

When endorsing a point of view, one should never be afraid to try something that has never been done before. Indeed, the more unusual, the better. Focus on what you want to be, think about the point of view and

Primark, Madrid – Store of the Future

let your imagination run wild. One of my favourite promotions is one I was involved with while I was at Saks Fifth Avenue, where we ran a 'Wild about Cashmere' event. I wanted the group to 'own' cashmere and that is what we did. As well as promoting our own designer collections, we also commissioned more than 250 original products to be designed in collaboration with some of Italy's top designers. The store was filled with everything cashmere, from cashmere sweaters and suits to cashmere-lined jewellery boxes and even cashmere skipping ropes. To promote the event, we tethered cashmere goats in Central Park and then had them led down Fifth Avenue. Everything we did was geared to getting customers to talk about cashmere and, of course, Saks. I don't think any retailer has ever before embarked on such an ambitious and creative approach to cashmere. By combining the world's finest fashion designers with one-of-a-kind merchandise, we succeeded in elevating cashmere to a lifestyle in a bold, statement-making way, which was a perfect match with the point of view of Saks.

CHAPTER CHECKOUT

✓ Lifestyle segmentation of the customer base is critically important.

✓ Pay attention to the basics, such as the look, feel and aroma of the store. It makes a significant difference.

✓ Windows are the eyes to the soul of a store. You can often gauge the health of a business just by looking at the standard of visual presentation in-store and in windows.

✓ Events and happenings bring theatre and discovery to a modern retailer's store – and that is what the customer of today is looking for.

✓ While the number of options in marketing has increased exponentially, there is no excuse not to use them effectively. The scattergun approach does not work and quickly gets ignored.

Chapter ten

OMNICHANNEL

One of my most eye-opening moments about just how far we've come in terms of ecommerce occurred during a family visit to Toronto. It was a couple of years after I'd moved on from my position as president of Holt Renfrew, where I'd spent just over five years. During that time, my wife Karen and I had made some very close friends in Canada and it was fantastic to return and spend time catching up.

One evening, we were having supper with two close friends and I took the opportunity to talk a little shop – I have a reputation for this. My friend's wife had always been a huge fan of Holt Renfrew and, being very wealthy, used to spend many thousands of dollars a year at the store. She'd always been a marvellous sounding board while I was determining the direction of Holts, so I was keen to hear her views on where it was now.

'Oh, well, I still love Holts,' she began.

The inevitable 'but' that seemed destined to follow this sentence hung in the air between us.

'But?' I prompted.

'I haven't bought anything there for I don't know how long,' she said, looking a little sheepish.

'But you were always such a fan,' I said. 'Where do you shop now?'

'Net-a-Porter,' she said with a shrug.

Then, sensing I'd be curious to know more, she went on: 'I have trouble sleeping. I always have. In recent months I have discovered the delights of all-night shopping!'

Everyone at the table laughed.

'Seriously, it's amazing,' she went on. 'I'll go online at 1am, look at all the clothes I like, order a few outfits and they are here, on my doorstep, the following day. It's changed my life! As you know, Holts have limited ecommerce, so while they have a lot of the brands I love, they don't sell them in the way I want to buy them.'

And there you have it. In a nutshell. Any retailer that ignores ecommerce does so at their own peril. The days when online shopping was an up-and-coming challenger to the high street and the preserve of a number of savvy specialist retailers are well and truly over. Ecommerce is, and has to be, at the heart of every retail business, and even venerable retail institutions must adapt and change to survive.

PROFESSIONAL VIEW
How to Be a Relevant Retailer

- Omnichannel cannot be 'omni' everything to everyone. We must provide a curated offering, online and in-store, that each customer feels is right for them.
- Retail is a social experience: a great escape and a place of discovery. Shopping at my favourite store is like seeing a Broadway show or concert. There is nothing like experiencing it live!
- The best ideas will involve both analytics and imagination. Data science is a necessity but cannot eliminate the soul of the retailer or the ability to dream about what hasn't been done before.

Tony Spring
Chairman and CEO, Bloomingdale's, USA

Mobility will allow for a perpetual connection with the customer. This relationship will require a balance of privacy, personalisation and frequency.

While bricks-and-mortar stores still have a vital role to play, stores need to match their physical presence with an online offer or risk losing out in a big way. As the conversation with my close friend proved, there has been a major shift in buying patterns. Customers are becoming ever more demanding and they want to shop in their way, at a time and place of their choosing.

Holt Renfrew began a limited online shopping presence in 2015, offering cosmetics, fragrance and skincare. Since then, they have expanded the range to include handbags and apparel.

There are very few retailers, large or small, that don't have some sort of online presence today. They have to. However enticing the in-store environment, it is a fact that internet sales are booming at the cost of direct-store purchases. Indeed, online sales are rising at 17% year on year.[20]

Even so, far too many retailers are failing to get to grips with the many challenges raised by the online environment. Despite more and more consumers turning to the internet to shop, some retailers are failing to deliver what customers expect in the digital age, let alone surprise and delight. With year-on-year double-digit growth, it makes business sense for us all to focus on capitalising on the potential that online offers.

CROWD PLEASER *ASOS, International*

During 2016, more than 20% of the UK population purchased something from the ASOS site, and it is easy to see why. This retailer has put the customer experience at the heart of its technology. The shopping site is easy to navigate, rewards customers for shopping with ASOS and makes it easy for customers to share their great experiences via social media. ASOS's YouTube channel has 70,000 subscribers and over 1000 videos, while its main Instagram account has over 4 million followers. ASOS maintains a style and beauty 'feed' on its main site, with up-to-the-minute tips. Plus, knowing that it has a predominantly young customer base, ASOS prioritises its mobile app, often upgrading it before the desktop website and using mobile-only promotions. As a result, 50% of customers shop via mobile phone, generating 60% of ASOS's overall revenue. If you want to sell to a young crowd, look at ASOS.

---

20   MRG, e-retail sales index, July 2016

Setting up and maintaining a viable online presence is no small challenge. It is expensive. In fact, it is a huge investment and ongoing advice is sometimes necessary. Digital technology is moving at such a pace that it is almost impossible to keep up, even for experienced operators.

At the very simplest level, there are many basic aspects to an online operation that retailers absolutely have to get right. Slow site speeds, particularly on product pages, drive customers crazy and can swiftly cause them to leave the site in search of a better experience elsewhere. Another area of frustration occurs at the checkout. Retailers that prioritise gathering customer data over a smooth and painless exit might find that their would-be customer gives up and leaves, abandoning their online trolley at the checkout. It should also go without saying that the quality and quantity of photos on site are a priority, since without a real-life sales assistant, the images have to do much of the work.

Getting even one aspect of the basics wrong will inevitably lead to customers giving up and going elsewhere.

Yet, what is it over and above the basics that gets an ecommerce site really buzzing? Don't forget, the myriad choices distracting the consumer are online too and there are a trillion distractions on the web, bombarding consumers with choices all the time. Arguably, too, it is easier to flit between web stores than to trawl through a handful of shops on the high street, making e-retail undoubtedly the most competitive environment of all.

The answer to how online stores attract, excite and enthuse the consumer is very similar to the way physical retailers should react: be creative, flexible, experimental and just a little unpredictable. Your retail website only has a matter of seconds to capture interest. We already know there is a huge amount of pressure on customers' time.

Ensuring your online presence is relevant and exciting can be a difficult balancing act. It is easy to get carried away by the thought of what can be done in the modern digital environment. You would be forgiven for imagining the number one priority here is to be hugely innovative and forward thinking to appeal to the tech-savvy consumer. The most cutting-edge e-retailer will always win when it comes to being relevant, right? When it comes to ecommerce, being way ahead of the crowd is not always the best place to be. In fact, it is possible to move too quickly and leave your customers far behind. They'll be too confused and nervous to order from you, which is clearly the opposite scenario from the one you are aiming for.

Remember, above all, a retail business is a commercial enterprise. The overall company is there to make money, not just to showcase the latest whizz-bang technology. In an ideal world, you'll take the customer on a journey and, thanks to tech innovations, be ahead of the pack.

RETAIL GRAVEYARD *Boo.com, International*

Five reasons why Boo.com became one of the most well-known fashion e-retail failures:

Too ambitious in its plans for instant global domination

Boo.com launched with ambitious plans to become a global sports retail site, a sort of sports and fashion version of Amazon. Therefore, it opened simultaneously in Europe and the USA. Amazon, on the other hand, established itself in one country, the USA, before seeking European distribution through acquisition and rebranding.

Emphasis on technology, not usability

The website opted for Flash-based navigation to dazzle and impress users, rather than thinking in terms of genuine customer needs. Even today, this would have made for a slow-loading site. Back in the dial-up days of 1998–2000, this was a terrible error. While analysts said it was the most clever web experience they'd seen, it didn't work well for ordinary customers.

Marketing was expensive and out of proportion with earnings

To build the Boo.com brand, a lavish online magazine called Boom was created. Boom required a large staff to cope with the many language versions required. However, it was not a catalogue that directly supported sales, and it competed with the large number of mainstream fashion magazines on the market.

The store's model clashed with established brands

Brand manufacturers had their own online sites and were reluctant to permit Boo.com to sell their wares at its proposed discount, thus cannibalising their own sales.

It tried to do too much, too soon

Boo.com's biggest fault was it tried to do too much at a time when customers were just beginning to come to terms with buying fashion online. When it launched, having spent several million on advertising, just 20% of UK households had access to the internet and those that did were on painfully slow connections.

PROFESSIONAL VIEW
How to Be a Relevant Retailer

- The history of retail is full of change, always brought on by a new concept that allows for cheaper pricing. What is next after ecommerce?
- The biggest challenge is to move from a product focus to a customer focus.
- The best defence is to own your offer and to keep it unique.
- History is a fight between distance and time. Time is always winning. To stay relevant, you have to be faster.
- Digital is a much bigger change than ecommerce. It is an opportunity to improve customer service.

Paul Delaoutre
Al-Futtaim, International

In the bid to become relevant, the virtual world is not too different from the physical one. The customer still wants to feel like an individual and they still want more than a simple transaction: they want to be entertained.

A robust ecommerce platform should focus on showcasing products and providing a simple means to buy them. In addition, to give it the edge, the ecommerce site should be easy to navigate, entertaining and absorbing for the customer. Don't be afraid of studying your close competition and basing at least some of your content on what they are doing. If they have discovered effective strategies, it stands to reason your shared customer base will feel comfortable using them, so don't try to reinvent the wheel.

At the same time, it is crucial not to be seen to be using the same old tried-and-tested strategies. To stand out and be relevant, a retail website needs personality and a point of view. Memorable brands *always* have a point of view. As I recounted in chapter three, when you think of a brand, you can instantly name its traits and characteristics: Coca Cola is friendly and fun; Mercedes is sophisticated, luxurious and wealthy; and ASOS is an engaging community for the lovers of the latest fashion trends. Very often those traits are naturally attributed to a brand by its customers, but it is possible to carve out the personality you want, particularly online.

Remember, though, that customers are increasingly looking for a new experience. They want something that makes them feel special and to believe they have purchased something unique. Personalisation has, quite rightly, been identified as crucial in the bid to optimise the customer experience online. Consumers want retailers to reach out to them on a personal basis.

Personalisation draws your customers into your online store because they want to experience something different from the norm. There are, however, two different options here. The first is to customise products to individual shoppers. Customisation can be anything from offering the facility to have, say, a name or logo embroidered onto an item all the way up to offering a service for a specialist bespoke product, where, say, buyers take their own measurements and bespoke garments are made. Bespoke has been proven to work successfully with a number of products, from bras to shoes.

Personalisation also plays a significant role in the marketing side online. It holds the key to how you *communicate* with customers, so they really feel you are reaching out to them as individuals.

This presents many challenges. Inherent in any online operation is the sheer quantity of data it gathers. The difficulty is: How do you use it cleverly? Think about a large-scale retailer, for example, which is an area where I have significant experience. Any retailer that a customer visits on even an occasional basis will soon have an enormous quantity of information about that person and their shopping habits. It will know, say, that they've recently moved house. This will not only be through the change of delivery address but also because that individual has ordered a large amount of home furnishings in the past year. Maybe someone in the family bought some lingerie in March, perhaps to coincide with a birthday or anniversary. Meanwhile, there will be intermittent purchases of cosmetics, kitchen equipment and school clothing. These purchases all provide clues and help to build up an interesting picture of the family involved.

The same goes for an online retailer, although the process is somewhat accelerated because the medium presents the perfect opportunity to ask a few questions along the way, which will add to the picture already being built by the customer's shopping habits.

The question any online retailer must ask themselves is this: How useful or accurate is this picture when it comes to communicating? Will I be using it in the best possible way?

Say, for example, a customer visits a lingerie store to buy something special for his wife to celebrate an anniversary. That retailer might naturally decide to focus its efforts around that anniversary. It might, for example, send a series of emails to the customer along the following lines: 'You bought this set last March – how about our all-new sexy two-piece this year?' Then the retailer might send another email about a new range for the spring. And another. For the overburdened shopper who never normally buys lingerie but did so just the once to mark a special date, the repeated communications about sexy bra-and-panty sets will be somewhat irritating. For the e-retailer, this presents a careful balance to be achieved. Communicate directly with the customer as an individual – but don't overdo it.

CROWD PLEASER *Thread.com, UK*

Thread.com is an online personal styling service for men that uses an innovative combination of personal stylists and a powerful algorithm to help customers choose between a large selection of over 200,000 items from around 1,000 brands. The idea is to take the best of what a human and a computer can do, for the best possible selection. When a customer signs up, they are asked a series of questions from which trouser fit they prefer to the price they usually pay for clothes. Customers submit photos of themselves and are assigned a personal stylist, who submits suggestions based on the answers and the software. The advice is pretty accurate, too – Thread.com has a 30% returns rate, meaning customers keep 70% of the choices made for them, which is a higher rate than that of other online pureplays.

It is a lot easier to communicate if the retailer can see a frequent and regular pattern of purchases. A coffee retailer like Starbucks will know all about your preferences. They'll even know that you drink Americano with skimmed milk every weekday of the year, except in the week before Christmas, when you treat yourself to a Double Double Fudge Bar Frappuccino with extra chocolate! Faced with a pattern like that, it is easy to communicate with a customer in a very personal way.

Financial institutions are well placed for this sort of highly targeted communication too. They have a vast amount of information about the customer and only a limited number of products to promote to them.

At its simplest level, every online retailer can use data to reach out to lapsed customers. Alarm bells should ring if any once-frequent customer suddenly disappears and doesn't come back. Every website should have a mechanism to alert the retailer to this possibility so a communication can be sent out to (a) find out what went wrong and (b) work on getting the lapsed customer back. I'm astonished that this rarely seems to happen. I was speaking to a colleague the other day who told me that he had stopped shopping with a well-known online grocer a few months earlier.

'I'd been shopping with them for more than five years, spending more than £100 a week buying my groceries,' he told me. 'I switched because their website was getting very clunky. I was amazed that no one got in touch to ask me why or to try to tempt me back.'

I was amazed too, but not entirely surprised. This sort of personal approach should be part and parcel of any online retail operation. E-retailers are superbly placed to spot these trends and do something about them. Why they don't is a mystery to me.

Personalised communication like this is a tad more difficult for large-scale stores and retailers in general, especially fashion stores. Customers don't buy those kinds of products with the frequency with which we buy a coffee or tea. Retailers in these sectors need to figure out how to communicate with customers in a personal but *meaningful* way.

I firmly believe that the secret to being meaningful lies in creating a community so that people feel part of the online store and involved with the brand. One very effective way to do this is to integrate the ecommerce strategy with social media.

There is a lot more to social media than simply pushing adverts and promotions. As ever, stores need to be a lot cleverer in their strategies and the customer needs to be at the focal point of any activity. The idea is to build rapport and shape your own online community. Firing off irrelevant messages, or posting too often, rapidly descends into the digital equivalent of cold calling. Retailers need to engage meaningfully without becoming a nuisance.

As always, there are different horses that are suitable for different courses when it comes to integrating social media with a personalised marketing strategy. Fashion seems to work best with Instagram, while anything targeting young mothers is best directed through Facebook. It might require a little trial and error to begin with, but if you already know your customer base a lot of it should be intuitive.

Social media ads provide one of the best opportunities to personalise customer engagement. The big networks, including Facebook, Twitter, LinkedIn and Instagram, offer a variety of advertising options. Effectively using these channels provides an additional touch point for both prospective and current customers to engage with your company.

Advancements in digital marketing technology continue to break the various marketing channels out of their silos, and social media is no exception. Marketers can increasingly incorporate data collected from other channels into their social marketing efforts. For example, if a prospective customer explores your website and visits a demo feature or a product page but doesn't complete the action, a pixel on the page can allow you to retarget that individual in a tweet or Facebook post with helpful content related to exactly where that person is in the buyer journey.

The key to getting it right in social media is to think social. OK, this sounds a bit obvious, but bear with me. Thinking social means understanding that most people generally do something because that's exactly what their friends do. The decisions and actions of others are seen to indicate the correct behaviour.

At its simplest, shops can take advantage of this by highlighting products that are popular on social media. Thus, Nordstrom has rolled out a programme of identifying top-pinned items from Pinterest in its online women's shoe and handbag ranges. It also creates a visual connection with its physical stores by making sure popular products in-store are flagged with the familiar 'P' logo.

We ran a phenomenally successful digital promotion for Hema for Easter 2016. The aim was to make the store *the* Easter destination and create interest in our selection of 16 differently flavoured eggs, which was the biggest range in the market. A state-of-the-art online Easter-egg-hunt game was created, where people could search for 16 eggs in a 360-degree digital world. Winners who collected all 16 eggs could pick up a free bag of chocolate eggs in-store. There was clear evidence customers loved playing the game, since the 105,000 who played spent an average of six minutes looking for the eggs. It was a great way to draw attention to the wide range of flavours too. Hema gave out 70,000 vouchers for free eggs, and 25% of people who submitted those vouchers went on to buy additional products.

Social media can be used to raise the excitement around a retailer too as well as create a closer personal connection. In the summer of 2016, J.Crew gave its 1.5 million Instagram followers a treat, launching its first-ever Instagram sale. Fifty pairs of pink sunglasses from the September 2016 collection were released a week ahead of the official launch and available only to Instagram followers. The sale was heavily flagged on J.Crew's website and teased in Instagram's 'Stories' feature, with messages to check back for more information. Such strategies instantly raise an online retailer way over and above the realms of being a simple transactional site that services the online community in much the same way as a physical store. They make it exciting and relevant.

Offering limited edition product to customers on social media channels makes those followers feel special because they are getting something first. It is a strategy that's been repeated by US fashion retailer Everlane, which uses Snapchat to make announcements and launch behind-the-scenes exclusives. In one campaign, Everlane introduced a secret shop with limited edition items that were only open to customers at specific times. Snapchat followers were helped to find the shop through a series of interactive tasks.

Which, of course, brings us to location. One of the most crucial aspects of e-retailing is location. It's often been said that the success of physical retail is down to location, location, location, whereas it is of no consequence to an online store since it can sell anywhere, anytime. However, this is not true at all. Location should also be a number one priority for an online store, regardless of how popular the brand might be already. When a customer searches for a certain type of product, any retailer selling that genre should be striving for the top slot on Google, or whichever search engine is used. Most customers won't scroll to the bottom of the page in a web search, let alone click to page two. Retailers spend a lot of money on ensuring the best possible web location and it is money well spent.

RELEVANT RETAILER *Boohoo.com, UK*

Five reasons why Boohoo.com has been a spectacular success:

Youthful, vibrant personality

Boohoo.com's corporate, visual and communications style imitates the youthful, vibrant fashionistas it wants to attract. From small beginnings in 2006, with just three staff at its headquarters in Manchester, UK, it has built a team of over 900 staff with the same age and lifestyle profile as its customer base. Everyone in the business is encouraged to send messages and images to the social media team to contribute to Boohoo as a social brand.

Regular updates

In keeping with its fashion-led profile, Boohoo constantly updates its website. The banner headline is used to great effect to entice visitors with new things, while various offers are used to tempt customers to buy that day. The range of offers is also a great way for Boohoo to quickly test and measure new trends.

Useful interactive features

Rather than just show static images, Boohoo plays videos of models wearing the item so customers can get a good idea of what it looks like when worn. Plus, Boohoo discreetly shows the model's measurements, so viewers can compare the look with their own size and shape.

Personalised email communications

Once a customer has bought from Boohoo, the retailer is skilful with its email communications, advising the customer of great offers that might interest them. The emails are highly targeted to match the style of the items, but they are personalised too. If a customer puts something in their basket but doesn't checkout, Boohoo follows up asking whether it can help. This is great on two counts: the customer feels that they are noticed and it gives Boohoo a chance to find out whether there is an issue with one of its products.

Original blog with interesting content

Boohoo has an interesting and varied blog. It promotes products, but not overly so, focusing more on a great mix of content that is of interest to its core customer.

The big question that many retailers grapple with is how to provide a smooth bridge between their physical and virtual shopping outlets. While much is said about the complete omnichannel experience, the truth is that the online side is often viewed as the enemy.

In some ways this might be understandable. A tremendous amount of my career has been spent at the helm of major large-scale stores and I know from experience that the internet, more than any other commercial operation, has diminished trading densities in the traditional department store model. Online retailers are now the go-to place for big-ticket items such as white electrical goods, furniture and furnishings, which were all once the bread and butter of large high street chains. There are fewer and fewer reasons to pay phenomenal town centre rents in order to be able to stock these items, when customers are just as happy to shop for them from the comfort of their living rooms.

For a while, department stores could at least feel comforted that they could fall back on their extensive range of brands in fashion and cosmetics, but even these products have been swept away in the internet surge. It turns out that brands are pretty good at selling themselves. And international brands such as Ralph Lauren, Burberry and Ted Baker have managed to build up far more comprehensive databases of dedicated fans than any department store is ever likely to do. To cap it all, the ubiquitous seller Amazon has climbed in on the act big time, delivering clothes and cosmetics the next day, or even the same day, for free.

The success of any omnichannel endeavour centres on leadership. In order to successfully link the aims, strategy and styles of physical and ecommerce operations, there needs to be a complete organisational change, and this has to be led from the top.

When any organisation beefs up an existing online operation to take centre stage, others in the business naturally become nervous, maybe even a little resentful. *There go my sales*, they think. Or, more pertinently, *there goes my sales incentive*. The people in-store withdraw into their silo and may even actively work against the interests of the online side of the business.

The way for ecommerce to work effectively as part of an omnichannel strategy is for a retailer's CEO to become its main sponsor. He or she has to be the most vocal, upfront, passionate supporter of the online side of the business. In most cases, it is necessary to reward sales staff in the physical stores for sales that are made online. It is easy to discern the exact location from where internet orders are made. Sales staff should then be allocated credit for each online sale secured in the immediate vicinity of their store – within, say, a radius of 15 kilometres. This will guarantee everyone gets behind the efforts of each selling medium, whether physical or digital. This is the way ecommerce and physical stores can become truly complementary.

Any chapter on technology would, of course, be remiss if it did not look forward to 'what next'. As always, Amazon is absolutely leading the way. Thanks to its innovative approach, the retail giant grew by $64 billion between 2010 and 2017. To put that into context, that is the combined 2016 revenues of Macy's, Nordstrom and Sears.

But many analysts are predicting that there is a *lot* more potential to be unleashed yet. In mid-2017, Amazon announced the strategic purchase of Whole Foods in the USA, Canada and the UK. Time will tell what the retailer's intention is.

Indeed, it has been said that Amazon's next innovation could *destroy* many brands and be the death knell for countless retailers. That innovation is Alexa. Right now, this 'intelligent personal assistant', which reacts to voice commands, is little more than an object of fascination in many households. It is mainly monopolised by kids who enjoy using it to get information for their homework or to play jokes. Fast forward two or three years, though, and many other retailers and brands may not be laughing.

The prediction is that Alexa will begin to use artificial intelligence to explore your buying habits and credit card history and predict what you will buy. There may be a service where, based on Alexa's algorithms, you can opt to be sent two boxes a week, one filled with what Alexa thinks you need and an empty one so you can return anything that wasn't quite right. You can recalibrate it as you go along: 'Alexa, we are having a barbecue on Sunday for eight people. Also send me three quotes for insurance on my 2017 Mitsubishi Outlander PHEV by email.'

You won't need to shop anywhere else. Ever again.

There is more too. Once consumers have adopted voice commands more readily (and they will), Alexa will have more say on the products they buy. If you are scrolling through, say, battery packs online, you will see dozens of different styles, sizes and brands. However, if you simply ask Alexa for a six-pack of double-A, there is nothing to prevent the device from offering Amazon's own brand as a preference. Indeed, there is already evidence that Alexa is favouring Amazon's own brand. To complete the loop, Amazon is (characteristically) throwing everything it has at this new stage in its development. The price of goods bought via Alexa is frequently lower than that of the same product bought on its website. Forget about those partnerships between stores and brands, painstakingly built up over the years. The algorithms are in charge today. At any one moment, Alexa might trade off one brand for another, for no other reason than its algorithm has just decided the original brand not the right fit for the customer, or Amazon, right now.

How do retailers, and indeed brands, compete against Amazon and Alexa? Well, relevancy and point of view are more important than ever before. Standing still simply isn't an option. On the plus side, there is evidence that people do still enjoy the interaction of a physical store. However, there needs to be a reason to go there and it must be supported by a strong online presence.

CHAPTER CHECKOUT

✓ Any retailer that does not have an online operation will lose out.

✓ Online services must amaze and enthuse just as much as their physical store counterparts, which means being creative, flexible, experimental and just a little unpredictable.

✓ Most importantly, there should be a smooth bridge between the online and physical shopping channels.

✓ Pureplay on its own needs bricks and mortar to support the customer's evolving needs.

✓ Amazon is a world force to be reckoned with. Ignore it at your peril.

Chapter eleven

INTERNATIONAL

I have spent my entire working career on the international retail stage. Indeed, for many years I barely set foot on home soil. I have seen first hand that it is possible to create a successful truly international retail brand, but it is also possible to become spectacularly unstuck.

On the face of it, it is easy to understand why any retailer might succumb to the lure of becoming a global brand. We've seen plenty of examples of brands, from H&M to Ted Baker to Hermes, that have succeeded in going global. Naturally, the thinking goes that any successful retail name should easily be able to reap the rewards offered by international expansion.

Not so. Globalisation is no panacea. Success rates vary wildly.

As anyone with an even passing interest in this sector will know, transporting successful retail concepts from one country to another is anything but clear cut. As many retailers have discovered, no matter how successful a brand is on home turf, you can't simply transplant it into another country and begin to count the profits. It doesn't work like that.

There are plenty of examples of fantastic brands that are runaway successes in their domestic market but that have failed spectacularly in some of their forays abroad. Take as an example Britain's largest supermarket group, Tesco. Tesco established its first US store in 2007, at a time when the chain was seemingly unassailable in anything it did. Commentators did mention the long list of British stores that had crashed and burned in their attempts to leap the pond (M&S, Dixons and HMV were all forced back across the Atlantic) but the feeling went that if anyone could do it, Tesco would be the one.

As we now know, Tesco was not the one to break the curse of a long line of British failures in America. In 2012, the supermarket admitted its American dream had been somewhat of a nightmare, as it set about unravelling its Fresh & Easy chain. This led many observers to question whether, if a player with the resources, scale and expertise of Tesco couldn't make it, who could?

To begin to answer that question, it might help to start by looking briefly at why Tesco didn't succeed in America. I believe its experience provides some vital clues to how brands should tackle crossing borders. Tesco's entrance to the US market was not without preparation: nearly 20 years of preparation in fact, including an intensive two-year period in which executives were sent to California to live with American families and observe how they shopped and ate. Sadly, though, Tesco appeared to ignore that research and instead set up the stores it was felt the market wanted rather than heeding what potential customers actually said – always a dangerous route.

In many cases, it was just little things that grated with the new customer base. US shoppers traditionally like to buy goods in bulk to save money. Fresh & Easy offered small pack sizes, similar to the ones Tesco sold in its domestic market. US shoppers value good service with plenty of human interaction. Fresh & Easy opened with banks of self-service tills. Presumably the thinking went that customers were being pushed towards self-service in the UK and seemed to be accepting it, so what is sauce for the goose is sauce for the gander, as they say. There were issues with the product ranges too: Fresh & Easy sold ready meals, which are highly recognisable to British shoppers but a largely unfamiliar concept in America.

To be fair to Tesco, it is not the only retailer in its sector to have tasted failure abroad. US grocery giant Walmart had to pull out of Germany and South Korea, while France's largest grocer, Carrefour, couldn't make it work in several European markets, including Austria, Germany, Norway, Portugal and the UK.

It is hard to say whether if Tesco had launched in more certain economic times it would have survived. My view is that the biggest mistake it made by far was not to pay enough attention to the planning and research it conducted among real potential core customers. Each country, whether

America, Australia or Austria, has its own sensitivities, cultural norms and preferences. Buying habits differ wherever you go. Understanding these differences is the key to success.

The secret to doing well on the international retail stage is no different from the secret to doing well on your home turf. No matter where in the world you are, it all comes down to one overarching number one priority: the customer. Get that right and everything else will follow. A brand that wishes to sell goods across a number of different global markets needs to focus on the customer and the local team in *each* individual market; if it does this, it won't go far wrong.

CROWD PLEASER *Net-a-Porter, International*

Without a doubt, the king, queen and Prince Charming of international retailing is Net-a-Porter. Global brands from Stella McCartney to Yves Saint Laurent to Alexander Wang all clamour to be on this site. Being stocked by this retailer not only guarantees new customers from around the globe but also gives a fashion brand value. Net-a-Porter has an enviable distribution network that services 170 countries and the content on its site is relevant to fashionistas everywhere. Founder Natalie Massenet was among the first to see that this is how we shop today, but she also capitalised on what interests the global customer, whether it is interactive magazine content, accessibility to must-have brands or simply a very fluid, vivid and fast shopping experience. Ask any fan (and there are many) about what they like about the brand and they'll invariably describe the excitement of receiving the black, sturdy box wrapped in grosgrain ribbon. Every time it is like unwrapping an eagerly anticipated gift, as they gently move aside the fine pink tissue paper to find an immaculate fashion piece. The entire range is fantastically curated and is widely accepted to offer the best choice of the best labels in the world.

The international perspective has, like so many things in retail today, changed markedly in recent times. Once again, our super-savvy customers are surging ahead, leading the way.

Just 20 years ago, as I toured the floors of shops and stores around the globe, it was not unusual to hear customers marvel at what they found there. Everything they saw was unfamiliar, from the brands to the way they were presented and sold to the stores themselves. 'Wow, look at that!' was a familiar refrain. Tourists would arrive in Japan and be blown away by the sights, sounds and smells of the food floors in the basement of department stores such as Takashimaya. Or, they'd tour New York's finest department stores wide eyed with wonder and disbelief at the vast array of colourful, stylish casual wear displayed in every size, shape and style imaginable. Bloomingdale's, for example, became the epicentre of retail theatre under the chairmanship of Marvin Traub, even attracting a visit from the Queen of the UK.

Over the years, things have changed – slowly at first and then accelerating at a dizzying pace. Today, many people don't think twice about hopping on a plane and going abroad. They'll regularly travel to far-flung lands that previous generations barely even dreamed about visiting even once in their lifetime. This gives everyone a whole new perspective on what they see when they tour their destination. Consequently, when the sushi bars and the coolest of cool brands set up in a new country, they'll need to work harder to impress their well-travelled customers. Plus, of course, many of these spectacles have travelled across the world too. They are now in a town near you, only a short drive away.

PROFESSIONAL VIEW
How to Be a Relevant Retailer

- Global societies are outpacing global companies in their adoption of innovation. Brands must embrace change or die.
- New platforms are enabling all brands, past and present, to have access to global markets, and these platforms must be fully maximised to enhance brand awareness/reach and commerce.
- Brands must no longer dictate communication to customers but embrace a two-way discussion.
- 'Pay it forward' in a manner that is relevant to the current generation, not in the manner you learned in the past.

William Kim
CEO, AllSaints, International

International

Whenever I talk to retailers that have international expansion in mind, I urge them to be cautious, plan well and do their homework. In my view, it is far better for a retailer to work on a country-by-country basis, focusing all of its efforts in each territory in which it opens, ensuring it is successful before trying the next. Rushing pell-mell into a world-domination strategy never ends well.

This country-by-country strategy has paid dividends for a number of global names. Japanese brand Uniqlo has a well-defined international expansion strategy. Taking one country at a time, it opens a show-stopping flagship store bang in the middle of one of the most fashionable shopping districts in the capital city of that market. In the USA, it opened in New York's Soho district and then on Fifth Avenue. The new flagship is merchandised to the gunnels with the very best of Uniqlo in terms of product, visual merchandising and store management. Wow factor? 100%. It is only when Uniqlo is satisfied that it has created enough 'noise' around the brand in each territory and the flagship is operating smoothly that it goes into the rollout phase.

I have found that a useful alternative to the 'flagship test' strategy is to test the retail brand out in an airport store in the target country. I call this a 'window to the world'. I have tried this a number of times in my career very successfully and it always provides lots of lessons to consider before making a major capital investment in a new territory. Airside in an airport is a hugely concentrated environment. Passengers have little else to do but shop, or eat and drink. However, competition is fierce, since there are many other stores in this limited area, all competing for a share of whatever passengers choose to spend before they jet off elsewhere. There are other challenges too. Even though you may be only dipping a toe into the water of a new country via your airport test, your supply chain strategy needs to be spot on. If you are not in stock of a particular size or shade, there is no way for the customer to come back tomorrow, nor will they be very interested to know you can organise for the item to be mailed to them. It is just too complicated for an impulse-buy scenario. No, product quality needs to be consistent and the supply regular. Those challenges notwithstanding, it is a great test of whether the customer responds well to a brand in a particular territory.

CROWD PLEASER *Victoria's Secret, International*

Victoria's Secret has long been the USA's largest retailer of lingerie and for many years fashionistas in the UK waited with bated breath for the range to arrive. I remember meeting the chairman, Les Wexner, a few years ago in Columbus, Ohio, and discussing international opportunities with him. He subsequently appeared to follow the travel retail route as a forerunner into various countries. When the company opened its flagship store in London's Bond Street, it featured everything from Victoria's Secret Pink to Victoria's Secret Designer collection. The store was set up as a feast for the eyes. Everywhere you turned you were surrounded by images of supermodels, and the staircase showcased a two-storey video screen showing footage from the brand's iconic shows and behind the scenes on commercials. I found the service to be immaculate and the assortments certainly appealed to the UK customer. Not surprisingly, the brand is already a huge hit in the UK.

Whichever entry point you choose, priority number one is getting to know your customer *before* you make your move. When entering new territories, it is very easy to make assumptions about markets, but this can end up costing a lot of money. Expanding internationally is never as simple as opening a store overseas and waiting for customers to turn up. There are countless things to think about, the most important of which is the question of whether or not there is a sufficient target customer base in the country (or countries) under consideration. Then, even if a customer base is thought to exist, is it absolutely certain there is a demand for a particular brand?

For fashion brands, there is an important question of sizing to consider too. In Germany, ladies tend to be taller than average. In Italy, many ladies are slender. In Japan, customers are, in the main, petite. If a fashion brand is unable to accommodate these variations – or decides to ignore them altogether, taking the one-size-fits-all approach – it will very quickly come unstuck.

Very often the safest markets to tackle first are those that most resemble the home territory, but, even then, this does not guarantee success. Any new market will never be absolutely identical to the one you know best, so the surest option is to make yourself as familiar with it as you can in order to ensure as smooth a ride as possible. My inclination is always to hire respected local expertise for an experienced opinion. Local hires are always a valuable source of knowledge on everything from trade barriers to culture.

Take, as an example, my experience with Hema, a modern Dutch variety-chain retailer operating over 700 stores across the Netherlands, Belgium, France, Germany, Spain and the UK. France has been a huge success with over 60 stores (at the time of going to print). The aim is to grow a substantial European store portfolio over the next few years.

It is important to begin from the stance that entering any new market is not a challenge that can be undertaken lightly. Apart from anything else, when a retailer enters a new country, it squares up against all the established players who are already there.

When Hema opened in the UK, it entered one of the most competitive retail environments on earth. British retailers have spent years honing their craft, understanding local preferences and responding to changes in customer needs. In many cases, the Hema Dutch range needed to be edited and aligned with British tastes. This was not to say that Brits would not take to 'unfamiliar' Dutch delicacies. Indeed, the UK's consumers have in recent years become a lot more adventurous. They have warmed in a very big way to Hema's most famous Dutch treats: honey *stroopwafels* (try them – you'll love them!). However, Hema's customers will not take to everything: often it is necessary to employ patience and trial and error. The important point is to share with your new customers the features and benefits of any unfamiliar products and, where food is concerned, set up tastings.

There are a lot of other opportunities international retailers can take to help themselves too. Collateral material in-store is another great way to lead customers to products they might never have tried before. Social media is important as well. Not everything will catch on, but it is possible to be very innovative so as to give each product the best possible chance of success.

In bringing Hema to the UK, there were seemingly inconsequential local differences to overcome. These disparities may seem obvious and thus easy to ignore, but they can and do make a difference between success and failure. Take Mother's Day as a case in point. Mother's Day is a great promotional opportunity for a business like Hema, which sells value, chic, well-designed goods that make fabulous gifts. Interestingly, though, Mother's Day is celebrated on different dates, depending upon which country you are in.

Similarly, the festive season is celebrated differently across the world. In the Netherlands, the most important day in the festive season is 5 December. This date in early December, just as UK shops are starting to shift gear into festive mode, is known as Sinterklaasavond (St Nicholas' Eve) and it is when Sinterklaas (St Nicholas) brings Dutch children their presents. In the UK, children need to wait until 25 December before they can open the presents left by Santa Claus during Christmas Eve. This is different again in Germany, where the most important day in the religious calendar is 24 December.

These are all critical nuggets of information when it comes to international relevance. They can so easily be overlooked in the rush to conquer new territory, but they can make a big difference, especially when trying to secure early wins. Retailers need to embrace this sort of local knowledge to plan their product assortments and promotional cycles. Without it, it is very easy to appear irrelevant and out of touch.

None of this should discourage retailers from moving into markets abroad. Yes, there are unique challenges, but, as I know first hand, there are rewards to be had too.

PROFESSIONAL VIEW
How to Be a Relevant Retailer

- Be the customer. Tech has disrupted how we connect, communicate and consume, but the consumer is not an alien species outside of our own comprehension. Connect to your own humanity, which is in all of us. Humanity has not fundamentally changed.

- Keep it simple, believe and trust only what makes sense to you, and always plan afresh. Don't be constrained by traditional mindsets and at the same time don't get caught up chasing the shiny new things.

- Truly believe in the value of all that you offer to make sure it moves your customer. The definition of 'experience' is evolving, so exploring and experimenting with what the definition of experience 'could be' will be the key differentiator in the future of retail. Being authentic in the product/service/content/experience offer provided to customers will be a prerequisite for any retailer.

> • The future of retail is about leading, not responding; build your power from the inside out. Retail success is created together. Teamwork and collaboration are critical for success. Invite the most brilliant people in the world to challenge, share and make real your vision of retail.
>
> *Jennifer Woo*
> *Chairman and CEO, Lane Crawford Joyce Group, Hong Kong*

Point of view is just as important as ever when working on an international basis. Customer expectations might be different in Spain or South Africa from what they are in the UK, but that simply means a retailer has to consider what it is that will set their brand apart on a country-by-country basis. The rules of the game are: get to know your customer (use local knowledge), decide what is unique about your brand and find a way to deliver this uniqueness. This might mean that a store in one territory looks entirely different from the same brand trading in another area, but that is fine. In fact, it might even be an advantage with our well-travelled consumers. A fashionista who regularly visits Paris, New York and London will enter her favourite store brand and be pulled up short by something completely new and unexpected. That's the wow factor we should all be constantly on the look-out for.

RELEVANT RETAILER *Ted Baker,* *International*

Five reasons why Ted Baker is an international favourite:

Strong brand identity

Ted Baker's international portfolio now numbers 448 stores and concessions, with 185 in the UK, 93 in Europe, 97 in the USA and Canada, 64 in the Middle East and Asia, and 9 in Australia. The brand has always been strong in airports, since it is just the right mix of affordability and luxury, but its real success is based on the strength of the brand and a relentless focus on design.

Ted Baker, Ottowa – Individual creativity in store design

Focus on British personality

Ted Baker capitalises on its British identity as it enters each new country, because that is what it knows its international fans like. It has won a reputation for setting, not following, trends with an individual, quirky viewpoint.

Unique store designs nod to each new market

The design of each Ted store is unique wherever it is in the world, and each one includes whimsical, humorous details inspired by the city in which it is located. The brand is well known for its creative window displays. Attention to detail is key.

Skilful marketing

Ted never advertises, relying instead on what founder Ray Kelvin calls 'Teducation', using guerrilla marketing tactics and taking advantage of social media. Digital screens in shop windows allow customers from all over the world to add their selfies to in-store activities such as the Vogue Fashion Night Out. Ted launched a highly successful shoppable short movie in the autumn of 2016 – 'Mission Impeccable', directed by Guy Ritchie.

Customer service a priority

Customer service is geared towards creating a memorable experience no matter where the retailer is operating in the world. Staff always strive to exceed expectations and create their own little piece of retail theatre.

If I were advising any retailer on how to become relevant in an international market, I would always advocate that they should make it a priority to ensure that they are bringing something different to that market. Since they won't be starting from scratch at the exact same time as other retail organisations, they are already at a disadvantage. Many high street rivals will have been around for years and will have established a reputation and rapport with their customer bases. Without something with a unique point of view, what is to encourage customers to leave the familiar embrace of these entrenched rivals? If you are simply offering more of the same, what is the point of going to all the expense and effort of crossing borders? You might be better off focusing your efforts in your own, established home market. Alternatively, I have found that it is important to bring some international flavour into your domestic stores.

Over the years in my career around the globe, I have found that it is essential to bring the best of the best to your speciality store.

As an example, here is a strategy I used to great effect during my time with German department store operator Karstadt. By the time I joined in early 2011, Karstadt was losing ground to leaner, fitter rivals, many of whom had come into Germany from abroad. The department store was becoming somewhat irrelevant. After taking stock and seeing how things were, we decided to inject some of my international retailing expertise into the flagging group to see whether we could re-ignite some interest in its home market. My strategy was based on four clear calls to action:

- Modernise the business to attract the younger customer.
- Differentiate through better and more innovative products.
- Sharpen processes and procedures.
- Simplify things so as to focus on what is important: the customer.

We decided the best way to get back the buzz around Karstadt was to offer customers new and exclusive international brands and merchandise assortments, something that was not common practice. Something entirely new and different would bring the best in international retailing right to their doorstep.

Innovation and differentiation are what appeal to customers. Promotions like these, which make the most of international influences and go beyond the norm, inspire people and turn stores into retail emporia of discovery and delight.

I would recommend to any retailer tackling an international strategy to think long and hard about the talent. As I outlined in chapter seven, your staff can make or break a business, and this is never more so than in the global arena. It is crucial to recruit staff who are local to the country. A localised workforce will come into its own as a store develops its point of view in each particular market. The leadership of the organisation may have strong ideas about how a brand tells its story, but it just might be that this story is completely at odds with local sensibilities. People in different countries place different values and priorities on different sectors of products, and only real locals will know this. For example, while consumers in many countries prefer to buy clothes and footwear in person, this is not always the case everywhere you go. In China, customers prefer to buy such things online.[21] Even payment method preferences differ wildly: in Japan, credit card payments are the norm, while in Germany customers are more likely to pay by PayPal, direct debit or bank wire transfer. Get any of these aspects of retailing wrong and you are in danger of being dismissed as irrelevant before you really get going. Again, there is no substitute for local knowledge when it comes to getting everything, even the smallest detail, just right.

---

21   Mintel. Haitao Shopping China, February 2017

International

Apart from anything, a local workforce will prevent a retailer from falling into any unfortunate communication traps. An inability to communicate properly with customers is one of the biggest barriers to international retailing. Stories abound of brands learning the hard way that their tried-and-tested slogans don't have the same meaning when translated into a foreign language. HSBC ran into trouble when attempting to promote its branches worldwide with the catch-all campaign 'Assume Nothing'. This translated into the somewhat less enticing 'Do Nothing' in a number of countries.

What many retailers with international aspirations might be asking themselves is: How do I ensure that my new workforce adheres to the hard-won principles of a brand? It is a legitimate concern. As the retail concept travels far and wide, it can feel more and more of a challenge to keep every member of a team in line. Plus, with so many of the workforce so far from the epicentre of the brand, how do you ensure that everyone is as excited about what you are trying to do as you are?

In 2013, in my role as CEO at Karstadt, I successfully set up Phase Eight's entry into Germany in collaboration with the UK-based fashion brand itself and the local German management team. Germany is a notoriously difficult market for many international fashion retailers. Not only does the customer have very strong views on what they want but there are also all sorts of sizing challenges, which means your stock control needs to be spot on. Management prudently began the expansion with just three test stores and spent a lot of time in the country in the build-up to the launch. What I most admired was what Phase Eight did in the weeks just before the three stores opened their doors. Every single member of staff recruited to work in the stores was brought over to London for five days. They were taken to Phase Eight's headquarters to be trained and spent time in stores. They were taken around London to get a feel for life in the fashion capital. They visited tourist hotspots, toured bustling shopping malls and took time simply mooching around. By the time they returned to Germany, they were walking on air. They *loved* Phase Eight, the management and its merchandise. When the stores finally opened in Germany, no one could believe how successful they were. However, when I spoke to some of the staff at the time, it was easy to see why. They were brimming over with enthusiasm. They told anyone who would listen how much they adored the brand and how wonderful the product was. Funnily enough, that enthusiasm rubbed off onto customers, who also lapped it up. It was a great launch and went on to become a very successful brand in Germany.

Following on from this, I would always recommend a localised website that caters to each country's language and shopping culture. There is nothing that will grate with customers more than looking up a store online and discovering a complete mismatch between the store they are learning to love and the one depicted on its own home page from a country they know little about. Build a locally focused website and it can be aggressively channelled towards the local customer base.

RETAIL GRAVEYARD *American Apparel, USA*

Five reasons why American Apparel's international expansion failed:

Expanded too fast

American Apparel holds the record for the fastest expansion in retail history. After opening its first stores in 2003, with stores in Los Angeles, New York and Montreal, it mushroomed into a global chain with more than 140 locations in 11 countries within three years. By 2009, that figure had doubled to 281 stores.

Loaded with debt

One of the implications of the rapid expansion was that the company was loaded with debt in order to fund the new store network. It was extremely vulnerable to changes in the market, competitor action and economic fluctuations.

Poor locations

Early on, American Apparel's success was helped by its choice of location, mainly in up-and-coming neighbourhoods where its target customer of young, fashionable shoppers lived. As the chain expanded, it became less focused, expanding into traditional shopping malls and clustering into multiple locations in a single city, many in high-rent areas. There seemed to be zero strategy in place for the choice of locations.

Ignored competitors

With all of its focus on building its store network, American Apparel seemed oblivious to the rise in popularity of fast-fashion rivals such as Zara and H&M. Indeed, American Apparel took the fight right to their doorsteps, making rapid inroads into the European market.

No differentiation

Even when shops were clustered close together, there was no effort to set them apart with different mixes of product. The retailer was faced with the double whammy of falling sales – because customers were no longer excited about the brand – and continually rising rents.

If you want to be successful as an international retailer, you need to invest in passionate local staff and put the time and energy into training them into the culture of the organisation. Understanding the culture of the brand is so often underestimated. It is also important to accept that not every brand will be an overnight success. Some retailers take years to establish themselves in a new market. Sometimes, however, if the appetite is there, you may be lucky and see returns from day one. Other times, you will need to plant the seed, tend it carefully and watch it slowly bear fruit. Plus, to be brutally frank, if a domestic business is not strong, it is a tough ask to expect the international business to be a huge success. To thrive in the global market, a retailer has to be the best of the best at home first.

PROFESSIONAL VIEW
How to Be a Relevant Retailer

- Personalised, genuine service is the most important differentiating element in retail. It is what builds true customer loyalty to a store, in a world where beautiful stores are countless and interesting products are available everywhere.
- Innovation on product through curation, interior design elements, customer-service-orientated features within the store, exciting visual merchandising, and add-on offers such as dining or art are all areas where innovation can be reflected.
- Curation is key to making a difference in a vast physical and digital market. A beautiful store in an excellent location, with great customer service, must have something interesting, new and unique to sell.
- Staying ahead means predicting customer needs and taking curation and in-store experience to the next level, well before other market players. Become regarded as an innovator, a trend setter and a pioneer.

Shireen El Khatib
CEO Fashion, Majid Al Futtaim, Middle East

CHAPTER CHECKOUT

The basic rules for international success are:

✓ Understand your customers and listen to them.

✓ Be prepared for the long haul.

✓ Get in a great team with local expertise and be prepared that not everything will work first time.

✓ Ensure you are relevant and competitive.

✓ Explain your concept to your customers.

ALMOST IS NOT GOOD ENOUGH

Many years ago, I attended a workshop held by Paul J. Meyer, widely believed to be one of the outstanding authorities in the fields of goal setting, motivation, time management and professional development. The time I spent there was as inspiring as I expected it to be but there was one particular philosophy that Paul shared that had a lasting influence on my career from that day forward. It was:

Whatever you can vividly imagine, ardently desire, sincerely believe and enthusiastically act upon must inevitably come to pass.

In other words, whatever you want to do, you can achieve. No goal is too big. This articulated something I had felt for years, but in such a neat way that I committed it to memory. In the years since, it has become somewhat of a mantra of mine. I have seen time and time again that, even when I have the most ambitious goals, they can be achieved. There is always a way. I believe this philosophy has contributed in great part to my success in the retail industry.

This philosophy is more relevant than ever today. There are so many challenges facing our industry. Competition is fiercer than ever. We have seen massive economic shifts, and new advances in technology are appearing at a breathtaking pace. We've no sooner got used to online when voice is already champing at the bit to succeed it, thanks to Amazon's Alexa. Someone asked me the other day about the speed of change in retail today and I drew a parallel with driving a car on the autobahn. As you are speeding along at 100 or more kilometres per hour, you notice a black speck in your rear-view mirror. Two minutes later, a car roars past at 200 kilometres per hour. That is the speed of change in retail today.

Customers are taking all the new ways to shop in their stride, soaking them up, and even keenly anticipating the next advance. There is no doubt at all that the customer is now firmly in the driving seat, and many shops are having to sprint just to keep up. Remember, the customer is now the 'superbeing'.

The only way to meet these challenges and to surprise and delight customers is to be relevant. Retailers need to embrace this brave new world and offer something new. Remaining with the status quo is not an option, nor is simply trying to do the best you can. As this book's title suggests, that is not going to cut it either. *Almost is not good enough*. There are many ways to achieve relevance, as I have illustrated in this book.

To conclude, I would like to summarise my points by sharing the top ten lessons of my career. I hope that they might, even in some small way, help to guide you towards your quest for relevance. While every retailer should forge their own path, these lessons should hopefully provide some inspiration in this quest.

So, without further ado, here are my top ten takeaways from a lifetime in retail:

1. Go big or go home

People have often told me that such and such or so and so can't be done, or that certain plans are too ambitious. I invariably disagree entirely. If you don't push things to their limits, you'll never know what can truly be achieved. And, as I have discovered through experience, most of the time you will only succeed if you do something in an authoritative way. Today in retail you have to make a statement. The fact that you have even tried something so audacious will count towards the wow factor too.

2. Execute ruthlessly

An idea is just an idea and a plan is just a plan until you make it happen. Don't fall into the trap of thinking big and leaving it at that. Be ruthless in the execution of your idea and surround yourself with people who are as aligned and committed as you are.

3. Manage inventory effectively

Without a doubt, the most important part of retail is the merchandise. As Ira Neimark says, 'If something is not selling, it is like a dead fish in a barrel. It stinks after a while.' Inventory management is more important than ever when customers have so many options to shop at their fingertips. You need the right goods at the right time, in the right quantity, at the right price.

4. Point of view is key

If you don't stand for something, you stand for nothing. A strong, well-developed point of view is essential. Create a vision of an in-store or online concept that is so different and compelling that others may try to copy it. Even if they do, it doesn't matter: you will have been the innovator. A shop with a strong point of view has a clear sense of what it is and, equally importantly, so do its customers. Define your point of view and articulate it. All the time. At every opportunity.

5. Nurture passionate talent

The most relevant retailers are the ones stuffed full with the teams who are the most passionate about what they do. These people are, without a doubt, any retailer's most important assets. Give people space to grow and develop, and allow them to make mistakes.

6. Embrace technology

Technology is critical to our success; customers love it and so should you. Find out how technology can transform what you offer, work with it and push it (and yourself) to the limits. Technology has a role to play in all areas of retail today, whether it is in marketing products, making the shopping experience more comfortable, or simply by making the experience so exciting a store instantly becomes the one everyone is talking about.

7. Embrace change

365 days a year. There is little point harking back to the old days. Or thinking wistfully about how things used to be done. Those days are gone. Take the best bits from days gone by, add what's happening right now and create something even better. And keep on doing it. Remember the best days are always ahead of us.

8. Joined-up thinking rules

Whether it is your marketing campaign, ecommerce site or physical store, make sure every aspect of the business is communicating with each other. It will become glaringly obvious if departments operate in silos or even begin to pull in opposite directions.

9. Global domination is no panacea

Don't even consider taking your retail brand onto the international stage until it is functioning well in the domestic market. Even then, proceed with caution, get to know each territory and work with people on the ground.

10 Understand your customers' wants, needs and desires

It is the customer who will decide whether a retailer is successful or not. This all-powerful superbeing is well informed, supremely confident and highly demanding. Everything, but everything, should be run through a filter that assesses how an idea will play out with the customer.

Don't be distracted by the naysayers who claim the end of retail as we know it is nigh. These are the same people who predicted the near total extinction of bricks-and-mortar stores. It is not going to happen. Customers love stores, shops and shopping malls, because they enjoy experience, discovery and innovation. Yes, changes are inevitable and there will be winners and losers, but if retailers act now they will be the winners in the long term. The ones who will get out in front are the retailers who put their energies into remaining relevant.

I have been asked many times about the future of department stores. Simply put, there is a terrific future for department stores provided they are omnichannel businesses that offer entertainment, discovery, innovation and great service. The challenge is not in the trophy stores around the world, such as Selfridges (UK), Harrods (UK), Bergdorf Goodman (New York), Lane Crawford (Hong Kong) or Le Bon Marché (Paris). These stores all stand for something and are customer focused. The challenge lies in making the 'thick middle' of department store groups relevant, energised and magnetic.

It is a natural reaction in times of great uncertainty to cut back and take a wait-and-see approach. I won't disagree that this is the time to be looking at the physical store estate to see whether the network of stores is too large or in the wrong locations. No doubt bricks and mortar will need to be trimmed substantially as ecommerce increases. However, I believe it is critically important to have a grand vision for what the omnichannel brand stands for. What is the strong point of view that will set it apart from the competition, and what does it stand for?

The focus of my attention has always been on creating a vision, communicating it to the team and then making it happen. Everything from merchandise assortment to store layout, ecommerce capability, inventory management, marketing, social media and of course customer service should be considered in this context. This is also the time to make sure marketing messages are spot on, and carefully targeted at individual customers to spread the word that you have not only the best product offerings in your category but also absolutely the best environment to buy them in.

None of this can happen in isolation. As I have said so many times already in this book, a motivated and passionate team is crucial to success. Lead them effectively, communicate the vision and see how they bring it to life. To this end, I would like to leave you with one final story.

In 1992, when I joined House of Fraser as CEO, the then owner, Ali Fayed, had some wise words for me. 'You can work like a demon,' he said, 'but you won't be able to do it yourself.'

He then pointed to a plaque that he kept on his desk. It said simply, 'There is no limit to what man can achieve, as long as he doesn't mind who gets the credit.'

He smiled and said, 'The problem with many business leaders is they get wound up about who gets the credit, so they keep things to themselves, try to do everything and end up doing nothing. You shouldn't worry about things like that. As long as the business is successful, that is all that counts. That way everyone gets credit for it too.'

Ali Fayed was absolutely right, of course. When House of Fraser was successfully floated on the London Stock Exchange, he presented me with an identical plaque. I still have it today and it makes me smile whenever I see it.

I will sign off with this final thought. The retailers that will succeed in this the most challenging of futures are those that show passion. As I have said, passion is the human soul on fire, and we all need that intensity to inspire customers.

Throughout my career, I have had people say to me, 'Andrew, we have *nearly* hit our budget.' Or, 'We *haven't quite* lined up those new designers to come in.' Or, '*Next year*, we will make that target number.' That is not going to cut it in the fast-moving industry that retail is today. (Indeed, I don't think it was ever acceptable.) We have to constantly say to ourselves: How can we exceed expectations? How can we do the truly extraordinary stuff?

And that extraordinary stuff is what is required to stay relevant, because, well, *almost is not good enough.*